LET
THE
TIDE
COME
IN!

LET THE TIDE COME IN!

C. Ernest Tatham

Creation House
Carol Stream, Illinois

First printing—August 1976
Second printing—February 1977

© 1976 by C. Ernest Tatham. All rights reserved.

Published by Creation House, 499 Gundersen Drive,
Carol Stream, Illinois, 60187
In Canada: Beacon Distributing Ltd.,
104 Consumers Drive, Whitby, Ontario L1N 5T3
In Australia: Oracle Australia, Ltd.,
18-26 Canterbury Road, Heathmont, Victoria 135

Biblical quotations from the *New American Standard Bible*
© 1971 are used with permission from the Lockman Foundation.

ISBN 0-88419-005-6
Library of Congress Catalog Card Number 76-16290
Printed in the United States of America

To

LOUISE

*who is not only a great wife,
but my long-suffering secretary
who typed and retyped the manuscript.*

Contents

Foreword

For fifty years C. Ernest Tatham has been one of conservative Christianity's articulate voices. He has gained renown among the Plymouth Brethren as a Bible teacher.

Then, at the age of seventy, following fifty years of teaching ministry, this profound Bible scholar moved into a new dimension of spiritual experience.

The Bible, he told me with tears in his eyes, that old familiar companion he had loved and lived with for all those years, had now come alive in his hands— bursting with startling, fresh truth. Some around him questioned his strange new freedom in worship, his new joy in life, his power in ministry. But no one could say he had denied his faith—he had just moved onto another plateau of Christian experience.

Few men come into such an experience as well-equipped as Ernie Tatham. How desperately this new generation of Spirit-filled enthusiasts needs his mature, Christ-centered teaching. I, for one, believe God has prepared this man for this time—to teach us how to keep our feet planted on the Word even though our heads are in the clouds.

Jamie Buckingham

Preface

It is embarrassing and humbling to admit that one has been wrong—especially when his position has calcified over the years. Well, mine wasn't quite calcified, for I had deliberately sought to keep it somewhat malleable.

Nevertheless I thought I knew what I believed about the use of spiritual gifts in the contemporary church. But during the past five or six years I have met some challenges that have jolted me into a reinvestigation of the New Testament. I saw the burgeoning spiritual phenomena, coming in everywhere like an irresistible tide.

Now forced to face up honestly to certain sticky New Testament passages that I had tended to piously duck, plus personal contacts with many believers who had met the Lord in a new and revolutionary way, I was compelled to reevaluate some pat answers. I had to thaw out and examine my tidy packages of deep-frozen theology. Not all will agree that my examination was what it should have been. Nevertheless I have tried to tell my story honestly.

Since God's Holy Spirit touched me in a new way, I have received many inquiries. Some have been friendly, some hostile, and some just curious. To these friends I owe some clear answers.

The position outlined here has not been reached hastily. I came to these conclusions only after a number of years of fresh investigation of the Scriptures and considerable reading on both sides of the subject.

As Paul would put it, "I speak as unto wise men: judge ye what I say."

Introduction

Recently, I was strolling along a lonely beach on one of the islands in the Bahamian chain.

The wide expanse of hard golden sand, the whisper of the Casuarinas, and the dancing translucent waters caught me in their spell. The tide was unusually low that day. At one spot I came upon several acres of exposed brown rock. Carefully, I picked my way over this jagged surface to examine more closely the exposed formation. The entire area was pock-marked with small pools that swarmed with tiny marine life. Stooping down, I began to interview the little creatures.

"How long have you been living here?" I asked boldly.

"Oh, for a long time," replied one, "ever since the tide went out."

"Well," I remarked, "I see that you are not alone You have plenty of neighbors just like you. Why, there's a pothole full of them right next to you here."

"But we have nothing whatever to do with them!" snapped one gregarious wiggler. "Those people left us, you know. We used to be all together, but they got mad and broke away when the tide went out."

"That's really too bad," I observed. "They look like you, they behave like you, and probably relish the same foods. In fact, I can't see any difference between you and them at all."

"But there *is* a difference," insisted my friend. "They are extremely shallow fellows, and really have no depth at all."

"What do you mean?"

"Well, look for yourself. Their pothole is only seven inches deep."

"And how deep is yours?" I inquired.

"Ours? Why, ours is eight and a half inches! In fact, we have one spot that is over nine."

I scratched my head in puzzlement while he continued, "But let me tell you something else. Those people are quite narrow, too."

"Narrow?" I asked.

"Sure. Their pool is only ten inches wide. *Ours* is eleven and a quarter!" The little swimmer swelled up as he made this significant pronouncement.

My curiosity now unrestrained, I chanced one more question.

"Say, what do you call your . . . your place here?"

"This, sir," and now he really did expand, "is the Atlantic Ocean!"

I picked my way back over the rocks.

High tide came in six hours later. Those acres of potholes were completely covered, and all those little creatures were swimming together again.

I looked and then cried, "Lord, send in Thy tide today!"

1

A Glance over the Shoulder

All of my Christian life has been spent in the fellowship of the Brethren[1] assemblies, whose virtues and weaknesses I have learned to appreciate.

My earliest memories cluster around two scenes—one a neat stone cottage on Norwich Street, the other a large hall above the Royal Bank on Wyndham Street in Guelph, Ontario, the city where I was born. At the cottage was a rope with which my mother would tether me to a verandah post in order to curb my wanderlust. And the lodge hall. There met the small "Exclusive Assembly" to which I was carried, and later led, Sunday after Sunday.

Known to us as The Meeting Room, the lodge hall was large, carpeted, and heavily scented with a most disagreeable odor. The hall contained several small platforms and lecterns. As a young boy, I often tried to divine the significance of the framed emblems and symbols that hung on the walls. The mystery of it all was too great, however, and I soon gave up.

Here in The Meeting Room, the faithful gathered each Sunday for the eleven o'clock Breaking of Bread and the evening Bible reading. Convinced that they alone possessed the Lord's Table, they were solemnly concerned to maintain its sanctity. The assembly consisted of Father and Mother, Uncle John and Aunt Eva, my maternal grandmother and Aunt Lula, my brother Sid, and cousins—Olive, Willie and Mamie. Oh yes, there was also a great uncle and a great aunt. In fact, only three members were not relatives. This family combine, which we called The Meeting or The Gathering, looked to my father as the leader. Father was recognized by Gatherings throughout the country as a distinguished Bible teacher and spiritual leader. This unusual respect rested upon him right up to his death.

One of the three non-relatives was a bachelor named John Mitchell. He had a small cancer on his lower lip, and in self-defense, a special communion cup was provided—a great concession indeed in view of the strong conviction that the common cup alone conformed to the Lord's appointed way! Watching this dear man reach out for his tumbler, following the dribble of wine down his chin, and the wipe of his soiled red handkerchief, never failed to awaken my compassion and my fascination Sunday after Sunday.

Except under extreme circumstances, my brother and I were never permitted to miss the morning meeting. But that regimen was somehow not applied to the evening Bible reading. So the memory of those solemn Communion Services was deeply etched on my young mind, and I concluded that here was the peak of Christian experience.

For us children, though, these services were lengthy and frequently tedious. Permitted to quietly draw pictures, we produced some strange scribblings during these sessions. But woe if we rattled the paper or squirmed too much! And so worship became a weekly endurance feat to which we submitted along with the other disciplines of family life.

Two recollections of these meetings particularly stand out. One Sunday morning my venerable, gray-bearded great uncle, after offering thanks at the Communion Table, accidentally upset the chalice, spilling the red wine all over the white tablecloth. Can I ever forget this dear man's embarrassment and how we boys struggled to stifle our mirth?

Then there was the solemn morning when we were visited by Mr. Michael Delaney, the corpulent Irish brother. As though it were yesterday, I recall him rising to minister the Word, and quickly departing from his text to embark on an excursion of personal anecdotes. His flashes of humor forced smiles on even the grave faces of Father and Uncle John. What a delight to hear him turn back the pages of his life and show us the spiritual struggles of his younger days. And all spiced with his fine Irish accent. But such breaks in the normal tedium were rare.

However, this weekly discipline was not without value. From the perspective of sixty years, I can bear witness that despite certain trifling oddities that marked this tiny exclusive company, spiritual impressions were fixed upon my heart that shall remain forever.

I recall our emphasis on the person and cross of Christ, the glories of His priesthood, and above all the imminence of His return. In this solemn atmosphere I learned the meaning of reverence. I could not escape the feeling that this little company, amidst all their severe austerity, was doing business with the Unseen. Theirs was no religious shadow-boxing; they were in the presence of One whom they knew and loved.

Dwelling upon the infinite value of the glorious obedience of the Father's Son, even unto death, for an hour every week gave me a strong foundation for later convictions. I shall be thankful for this always. It could never be charged that, in this case, the packaging obscured the content, for there really was no packaging at all. Perhaps our a capella singing was less than harmonic, but the words of those scriptural and worshipful hymns became an early part of me—spiritual spoil that would enrich my entire Christian life.

If these obscure believers had their strengths, they also had weaknesses. And serious weaknesses they were. The Gathering's eventual death and disintegration suggested that irrelevant elements were already working in those early days.

First, ingrown thinking impregnated the whole atmosphere. The text I heard most frequently was the precious promise of Matthew 18:20, "For where two or three have gathered together in My name, there I am in their midst." I was given the impression that here lay the justification for our remaining in the "two or three" category, and that the Lord would be displeased should we outgrow this dimension. Our two-or-three philosophy encouraged small thinking; small thinking issued in small aims; small aims yielded small results. How different might have been the outcome had we balanced Matthew 18:20 with Acts 4:32: "The multitude of them that believed" (KJV). These dear folk, however, could never be charged with a lack of other-worldliness. If overdoing this virtue were possible, they certainly pressed toward the furthest boundaries. For they had little communication with a perishing world. Heavy on worship, they were light on witness. Our haven insulated these brethren from the Christless masses that marched past the Room on sidewalks below. There was no evangelistic outreach. Not that these Christians had disavowed evangelism; they had not. On the contrary, Father occasionally ventured onto the street corner alone to proclaim the Good News—alone because timidity or apathy had seized the rest of our little flock, and none came to support him.

But there may have been a more subtle reason. Had not the Lord placed worship before service? Was not the upbuilding of saints really more important than the conversion of sinners? Did not the breaking of bread and Bible study deserve higher priority than preaching the Gospel? After all, God could use the Open Brethren or even the Salvation Army to preach on the street corner. True, a couple of devoted and courageous ladies made attempts at a home Sunday School. But these had petered out.

Some of our young people drifted into the world upon reaching adolescence. I was one of these. When

21

Father died during my early teens, Mother seemed to lose her grip on me and away I plunged for three turbulent years.

Much later I observed that if we as believers don't *go* out to witness to our faith, we will *die* out. And die out that little company did. Such a doom is the inexorable result of spiritual childlessness.

The lesson is plain. Devotion to God must be balanced by ministry to man in evangelism and missions. If worship is genuine, witness will be fervent. One hand, filled with incense, will reach up to the throne while the other, filled with heaven's bread, will reach out to a lost and hungry world.

FOOTNOTES

1. The Brethren, often dubbed Plymouth Brethren, are a loose association of independent local congregations which date back to 1830. Thoroughly conservative and evangelical in doctrine, they reject clerical officialism and strive to maintain organizational simplicity.

2

The Tent on Sleeman's Flats

"The Holy Rollers have hit town. They're in a tent down on Sleeman's Flats."

"Hey, let's go see what's going on." This exciting information came from my teenage pals Sam Stewart and Alex Irvine. The three of us had been reared in fervent Brethren homes, though none of us had personally met the Savior at that point. Yet, we possessed a fair amount of theological smugness. As a trio of budding young Pharisees, our rating wasn't bad!

"Who are the Holy Rollers?" I asked.

"Well, maybe they call themselves 'Pentecostals' or something like that. But I hear that they roll, clap, sing and shout. That's how they got their name." said Sam.

"That's not all," Alex interjected. "The preacher is a *woman!*"

A woman preacher?

Wow! We all knew *that* was unscriptural. What fun this spectacle would be!

The tent was neither large nor elegantly equipped. The benches were crude and the platform simply furnished with a lectern, a few chairs, and a wheezy pump organ. Mrs. Sharp, a buxom middle-aged woman, was the evangelist. She appeared to be running her Gospel campaign singlehandedly. She preached, prayed, sang, and pumped that reluctant organ between puffs and droplets of perspiration. Hecklers lay on the grass around the open flaps and mocked with unholy glee especially at an outburst of tongues or prophecy.

We three young fellows missed few meetings that summer. Those services were never dull. They crackled with the unusual—a blend of fervent evangelism, shoutings, strange languages, excited outcries, and plenty of laughter.

At times we were honestly impressed by Mrs. Sharp's evangelistic earnestness. Always, we were amused by her platform gyrations reinforced by loud denunciations of the Devil, whom she recognized as a nightly member of the audience.

One evening we were stunned at the sight of a man moving around the tent brandishing a stick and shouting for the Devil to leave at once! On another occasion a man was literally propelled from his seat two or three feet into the air, as by an electric shock, as he shouted wildly, "Glory"!

Nor will I forget that late hour when three or four women stood sobbing and shaking in a united paroxysm of noisy emotion. Their hair, once arranged in tidy buns, hung in disarray around their shoulders because of their swayings. Their sleepy children cried at their sides. On another evening we saw a man crawl around on his stomach and mutter incoherently. And once a new male convert actually jumped over the stove!

But Mrs. Sharp did preach clearly God's way of salvation through the Lord Jesus Christ. I still recall a message she gave comparing Noah's Ark to the Savior who took the storm of judgment on our behalf, and who provides safety for all who trust Him. And she always stressed the urgency of the hour in view of the Lord's return to remove His church. For us, it was all a mixed bag of the familiar Gospel draped in a new wardrobe of bizarre emotion and strange tongues.

The following year, 1921, brought revolutionary changes into all our lives. Each of us came to know the Lord Jesus Christ as Savior of our souls. The Christ we had heard about as an important historical figure now became a living person to us as each, in turn, opened his heart and life to the man of Calvary, the Lord of glory. Shortly after our conversions, we were baptized and received into assembly fellowship. This assembly was less exclusive than the one I had known in earlier years.

What glorious weeks followed! The Bible became a new book, and the fellowship we discovered with other new Christians opened an entirely new dimension of living.

I have always been a book lover. Now my appetite turned to the Scriptures, and I ravenously devoured them. It seemed that I could not get enough of either the Word of God or fellowship with God's people. How thankful we were for the men who guided our little assembly, who opened the Scriptures to us at Tuesday evening Bible studies, and who helped us over the hard spots. They loved us, and we knew it.

By now the Pentecostals had a permanent beachhead in our town, and were meeting regularly in a shabby upper room on a side street. When there were no meetings in our Hall, we three fellows would often attend their lively services.

The format continued much like the one we had witnessed in the tent, but without the lady preacher. Our interest and curiosity grew. We even questioned these people, but their answers often left us floundering.

Acts 19:1-2 was one of their favorite texts, and I was usually sore pressed for a satisfying explanation. Just what did Paul's strange question mean? Among other thorny passages they threw at us was Acts-two-and-four, the cornerstone text, which we felt a bit more confident to handle.

We had only one thing to do: unload these sticky questions on our Brethren teachers—both the local men and the visitors. Did we get answers? Quickly and decisively. And it was easy to detect their disapproval of our contact with those misled people and their dangerous doctrines.

The Tuesday evening Bible studies at the Hall now acquired a keener edge. Difficult questions were aired; the elders tackled them courageously.

The sign gifts such as miracles, tongues, prophesyings, and exorcisms, they explained, were divine manifestations given to corroborate the new message of Christianity at the beginning of the dispensation.

Because they were primarily directed to the Jews, and thus coterminous with that probationary period, they were withdrawn at the close of the apostolic era when Israel's rejection became official and final. For support they drew on Hebrews 2:3, 4: ". . . . so great a salvation? After it was at the first spoken through the Lord, it was confirmed to us by those who heard, God also bearing witness with them, both by signs and wonders and by various miracles and by gifts of the Holy Spirit according to His own will."

We concluded that miraculous confirmation was necessary for and limited to those who had personally known the Lord Jesus. Furthermore, although the period covered by the Book of Acts was ushered in by a mighty gush of miracles, these wonders receded as a sort of ebb-tide toward the close of the same book. They did a quiet fade-out as Paul's ministry concluded and the apostolic period closed. In the words of I Corinthians 13:10, "the perfect" had come with the completed Scriptures; prophesyings were no longer necessary.

"But," we asked, "what of the other miracle gifts and supernatural enablements available to Christ's body and catalogued in I Corinthians 12?"

Again, the answer was quick and precise. "Most of these should also be regarded as passé, if only because many centuries have elapsed since the Christian church possessed them. Was it not obvious that these gifts had been withdrawn by the Church's Head?"

A special word of caution came for what the Scriptures described as "tongues." Tongues, we learned, were divine vehicles for preaching the Gospel to foreigners, such as on the day of Pentecost. This spiritual gift rendered language study unnecessary during that period, and that period only. Anyone who *really* had the gift of tongues today would prove his claim by marching into the foreign-speaking enclaves of our large cities and fluently proclaiming the Gospel to these people in their various dialects!

With these pronouncements, we young men were urged to forget the Pentecostals. Further contact would not only be condoning serious error, but also exposing ourselves to demonic delusions. Since Satan transforms himself into an angel of light, it should be no surprise if his ministers transform themselves into the ministers of righteousness (2 Corinthians 11:13-15).

In the face of these condemnations, we now had serious misgivings, if not deep apprehensions about our previous observations. Evidently we had witnessed satanic counterfeits, all the more deadly because they paraded under the guise of genuine evangelism and Biblical Christianity. Those folks were deluded fanatics; their products were religious contraband.

Our interest was pretty well finished. Henceforth we would stay closer to harbor and attend our own meetings.

But a troupe of question marks still danced on the backstage of my mind. I wondered.

3

"Please Write a Course
on the Holy Spirit"

It was 1942. The Second World War was raging, and
servicemen were asking for more information on the
Christian faith. Dr. R. E. Harlow, who with John Smart
and me had fathered the Emmaus Bible School the
previous year in Toronto, Canada, felt that the wide
acceptance given to a few previously written elemen-
tary correspondence courses might provide a good
vehicle to bring help and encouragement to men in the
service and their loved ones at home. He was concerned
that teaching on the person and the work of the Holy
Spirit was greatly needed.

There was at that time a tendency to leave this particular subject to the Pentecostals, who were regarded

by some as specialists in the field. Other evangelicals were skittish about it, avoiding anything that smelt of religious emotionalism.

I had already given lectures on this subject to our evening school. Now it appeared that I should commit this material to paper and release it to the growing list of Emmaus Correspondence Course students. The task was formidable in terms of time and research, and also because it would become the official position of the school. It must have the proper balance of theological depth and accuracy on the one hand, clarity and simplicity on the other.

After some consultations, we agreed that I would write the text for the twelve-lesson course. Dr. Harlow would prepare the companion tests.

Busy weeks followed. I lectured daily at the school, found time for our five children at home, and preached in several local Brethren assemblies as well. But the assignment proved exhilarating; days flew by swiftly.

The new course was built around two main pillars: the Spirit's person and His ministry. The title of the text eventually became "The Holy Spirit at Work." The text is still available from Emmaus Bible School in Oak Park, Ill.

I had long known and taught that the New Testament emphatically declares the full deity of the Comforter. He is God, and possesses all of the attributes of divine being—eternal existence, omniscience, omnipotence and omnipresence. As "the eternal Spirit" (Hebrew 9:14), He ranks as equal of both Father and Son, for such an adjective as *eternal* could never be applied to a mere transient creature.

As *omniscient* He is all-knowing, the Spirit of Jehovah, wisdom and understanding, counsel and might, knowledge and the fear of the Lord (Isaiah 11:2). He searches all things, yes, the deep things of God, things that are beyond the grasp of the most brilliant intellect. Not only does He search and research these divine depths, but He also communicates them to us—providing we are tuned in. True spirituality is the price-tag of divine wisdom and knowledge. The heavenly Teacher never shares His goodness with carnal Christians. To receive these spiritual luxuries we must be tuned to God's wavelength (I Corinthians 2:9-16).

He is also *omnipotent*—all powerful. At the birth of planet earth He exerted His creative might, reducing chaos to cosmos, garnished the heavens and communicated life to man (Genesis 1:1-4; Job 26:13; 33:4; Psalm 104:30). His divine energies are also demonstrated in His miraculous transportation of Philip the evangelist from the Gaza desert to the City of Azotus (Acts 8:39, 40). But more astonishing was His raising of our Lord's body from death. Peter informs us that Jesus was made alive by the Spirit (I Peter 3:18).

And the great Comforter is *omnipresent*. He is everywhere. No geographical spot is off-limits to Him. "The seven Spirits of God, sent out into all the earth" (Revelation 5:6) are not numerically different but rather one person who moves within a sevenfold plenitude of operation, reaching into the most remote corners of earth.

Atheistic governments may expel the evangelical missionary, but no government can order out the Holy Ghost. The Psalmist exclaims: "Where can I go from Thy Spirit? Or where can I flee from Thy presence? If I ascend to heaven, Thou art there; If I make my bed in Sheol, behold, Thou art there. If I take the wings of the dawn, If I dwell in the remotest part of the sea, Even there Thy hand will lead me, And Thy right hand will lay hold of me. If, I say, 'Surely the darkness will overwhelm me, And the light around me will be night,' Even the darkness is not dark to Thee, And the night is as bright as the day. Darkness and light are alike to Thee" (Psalm 139:7-12).

But do the Scriptures ever actually refer to the Spirit as God? Indeed yes. In the sobering story of Ananias and Sapphira, Peter accuses the former of lying to the Holy Spirit, and then follows up with the charge, "You have not lied to men, but to God" (Acts 5:4,5).

As further evidence of His deity, He takes His place as an equal with the Father and the Son in the Christian baptismal formula, and in the well-known apostolic benediction (Matthew 28:19; 2 Corinthians 13:14).

Just imagine the whopping shock if we were to read that Christ's disciples were to be baptized in the name of the Father, the Son, and Isaiah! Or that the grace of the Lord Jesus Christ and the love of God were to be energized by the communion of Michael the archangel!

Would we not instantly shout our objection: "But this makes both Isaiah and Michael equal with the Father and the Son!" And we would be right. The fact that the Spirit is named with the other members of the Godhead proves His deity and equality.

Furthermore, He is a real person—just as complete a person as the Father and the Son. A person does not necessarily possess a human body. The existence of angels demonstrates this. Personality, whether divine or human, means the coordinated function of intellect, emotion, and will. By the intellect comes knowledge; by the emotions come feelings; and by the will come both decisions and actions.

Now apply this criteria to the Spirit, in light of I Corinthians 2:10-12: "But God hath revealed them unto us by his Spirit: for the Spirit searcheth all things, yea, the deep things of God. For what man knoweth the things of a man, save the spirit of man which is in him. Even so the things of God knoweth no man, but the Spirit of God. Now we have received, not the spirit of the world, but the spirit which is of God; that we might know the things that are freely given to us of God." Not only does the Spirit possess infinite intelligence, but He communicates some of this heavenly knowledge to us as we manifest the capacity to receive it.

As for the emotional element, we need refer only to His love, His grievings, His yearnings, or His disapprovals (Romans 5:5; 15:30; Ephesians 4:30; Acts 16:6, 7; Hebrews 10:29). Furthermore, His will is evidenced by the fact that He leads (Romans 8:14; Galatians 5:18), makes alive (Romans 8:11), teaches (John 14:26), sanctifies (I Corinthians 6:11), and sometimes even smites (Acts 5:4, 5).

As I poured over the Scriptures in my study I was overwhelmed at the variety of ministries of the Holy Spirit. I decided to concentrate on the four that dominate: His ministry to Christ, to the world, to the Church, and to you and me as individual Christians.

HIS MINISTRY TO CHRIST

We all have seen brilliant floodlights on a prominent building or monument at night. Cleverly concealed in the lawn, the powerful electric lamps throw their beams so that our attention is focused upon the object lighted rather than upon the source of the light. In fact, we are usually not at all interested in where the light is coming from. We merely look at the lighted object.

In relation to Jesus, the Holy Spirit is the greatest of all witnesses, for He focuses His powerful spotlight on Him in order to attract attention to His beauty and glory.

In that intimate Upper Room ministry (John 13-17) our Lord allayed the rising fears of His beloved followers by promising not to leave them orphans, but to come to them (John 14:18). Minutes earlier He had promised to return *for* them (verse 3); now He promises to return *to* them. The listeners at that time probably did not fully understand. But we who live on this side of the cross and resurrection readily recognize that Jesus Christ did come again in the person of the descending Spirit at Pentecost, henceforth to live in and operate through them, His church and body. "When the Helper comes . . . that is the Spirit of truth, who proceeds from the Father, He will bear witness of me. . . . He shall glorify Me; for he shall take of Mine, and shall disclose it to you" (John 15:26; 16:14).

Just as the Lord Jesus witnessed to and magnified the Father, the Spirit now bears testimony to and glorifies Jesus by displaying His worth and work through us. The Spirit would draw attention to neither Himself nor us. The channels are not important; Jesus Christ alone is to be honored.

HIS MINISTRY TO THE WORLD

John records the details of the Lord's Upper Room ministry. Given only hours before His execution, His Gospel contains more vital data on the Holy Spirit's ministry than the other three put together. This suggests how urgent the subject was to Him, how supremely important for His disciples to know as much

34

as possible about their new Guide. Not only would the Spirit assure the disciples of their continuing relationship with the risen Jesus, but He would also speak in stern conviction to a Christ-hating world through them. ·

Our Lord's announcement of these things must have fallen on their ears like a thunderclap.

"It is expedient for you," said Jesus, "that I go away" (John 16:7 KJV).

We probably would have shouted out, "No, Lord, don't . . ."

But wait, He hasn't finished. "Nevertheless I tell you the truth, it is expedient for you that I go away: for if I go not away, the Comforter will not come unto you; but if I depart, I will send Him unto you. And when He is come, he will reprove the world of sin, and of righteousness, and of judgment: of sin, because they believe not on me; of righteousness, because I go to my Father, and ye see me no more; of judgment, because the prince of this world is judged."

The last two words of verse seven, "unto you," show that the Spirit would not reprove sinners by shouting Bible texts from the clouds, but would speak through flesh-and-blood. Men and women would be His tools to bring conviction of guilt. This is still His method. He uses believers in the preparatory work of saving the lost.

The word *reprove* (v. 8) is used in John 3:20 in the sense of "discovered." "For every one that doeth evil hateth the light, neither cometh to the light, lest his deeds should be reproved." In Ephesians, the same word is translated "exposed" (chapter 5:11 NASB). Reproof, conviction, discovery, and exposure, therefore, are the Spirit's means of showing the sinner his need. Clearly, it appeared to me, just as the seamstress's needle pierces the cloth to draw through the thread, just as the surgeon's scalpel makes the incision, just as the plow breaks the hard soil—so the heavenly Convictor initiates the work of repentance and faith in our Lord Jesus Christ. He convicts of sin, righteousness, and judgment, and He does it through us. But we must be yielded and available, for He does not coerce. He impels but does not compel.

The more I pondered these great truths the more excited I became as I realized afresh that God the Spirit wants to speak through us today—through both our lives and our lips! Would we let Him?

4

Baptism of the Spirit: Individual Attainment or Corporate Accomplishment?

After looking at the Spirit's ministry to Christ and to the world, I began to study and write of it in relation to the Body of Christ.

HIS MINISTRY TO THE CHURCH

I saw plainly that the true Church of Jesus Christ is the aggregate of all true believers.

The ascended Christ is the Head, and the Holy Spirit animates and unifies the members of the Body. Jew and Gentile—racially, culturally and religiously at swordspoint—find in Christ a common unity of life and love. "For He Himself is our peace, who made both groups into one, and broke down the barrier of the dividing wall, by abolishing in His flesh the enmity, which is the law of commandments contained in ordinances, that in Himself He might make the two into one new man, thus establishing peace, and might reconcile them both in one body to God through the cross, by it having put to death the enmity. And He came and preached peace to you who were far away, and peace to those who were near; for through Him we both have our access in one Spirit to the Father" (Ephesians 2:14-18).

The baptism of the Holy Spirit effects this oneness. But here I entered the arena of heated controversy. Even in the days before the current revival of interest in the person and work of the Holy Spirit, there were two different viewpoints.

First, is that the baptism is an individual experience to be sought by every Christian who would have God's best. Second, the baptism is a corporate action that occurred at the outset of Christianity and which resulted in the formation of the Church.

I determined to consider these views separately.

"Receiving the baptism" is a common phrase used by thousands to describe the believer's initial encounter with the Spirit of God. Sometimes this encounter is emotional though unspectacular. At other times it is followed by speaking in other languages or "tongues" or prophecy. Some circles urge believers to pursue this experience. Until it is attained, the believer is deficient in spiritual privilege and power. He may be baptized in water, but still unbaptized in the Spirit.

I was troubled. Would this position bear the scrutiny of the New Testament, I wondered.

The answer did not appear difficult, for the Bible contains only seven references to this ministry (Matthew

3:11; Mark 1:8; Luke 3:16; John 1:33; Acts 1:5; 11:15, 16; and I Corinthians 12:13).

It was clear to me that the first four of these were predictions by John the Baptist, the fifth by the risen Lord, the sixth by Peter, and the seventh by Paul.

Furthermore, the first five all point to the future, "He *shall* baptize you with the Holy Ghost, and with fire" (KJV). The last two point backward into the past. (In the I Corinthians 12:13 passage the NASB and others translate, "we *were* all baptized.") From this I could only conclude that the baptism in or by the Holy Spirit occurred on the day of Pentecost for Jewish believers. Later, Gentile converts experienced the same mighty outpouring in the house of Cornelius (Acts 10). Wasn't it significant that of these seven references, only one really *explains* what this baptism actually is? The other six speak of it, but do not explain it. I Corinthians 12:13 alone does so. "For by one Spirit we were all baptized into one body, whether Jews or Greeks, whether slaves or free, and we were all made to drink of one Spirit."

But I also noted that not one of these Corinthians was a Christian at the time of that first memorable Pentecost. Yet Paul says that *all* of them had been baptized with or in the Holy Spirit, and that in spite of their notorious carnalities!

Now the question arose as to just *when* that took place? Was it when each individual Corinthian believer sought and found an experience with the Spirit, and was this encounter ratified by tongues-speaking? If so, then it is difficult to understand Paul's desire that they all speak with tongues (I Corinthians 14:5).

I had already seen in this same epistle that Paul

39

states: "Our fathers were all under the cloud, and all passed through the sea; and all were baptized into Moses" (I Corinthians 10:1, 2). To whom do these "fathers" refer? Who were they? Surely they were those Israeli patriarchs who came out of Egypt. However, hundreds of years later Isaiah referred to their descendants as "our fathers" (Acts 28:25, 26). A late Old Testament prophet declared to the people of his day, "It was I who brought you up from the land of Egypt, and I led you in the wilderness forty years" (Amos 2:10).

But these people had never been in Egypt or the wilderness! Yet they all shared in both experiences. The simple explanation, of course, appeared to be in the racial continuity and identity between them. In this identity they all shared in those historical experiences.

Could this same principle of spiritual identity explain how the Corinthians had already been baptized by the Spirit into Christ's Body?

If I were to assume that we Americans received our independence from the British Crown in 1776, I would be assuming a fact. No one seriously believes that because he was not alive in 1776, he is still a British subject.

The three great ethnic groups invaded by Christianity at and following the first historic Pentecost were Jews, Samaritans and Gentiles. Acts 2 records the Jewish visitation, Acts 8 the Samaritan, and Acts 10 the Gentile. Each group in turn received salvation, water baptism and the Holy Spirit. By the Spirit's baptism, these three rival and hostile communities were corporately immersed into one organic whole. In later days, when individuals were saved, they were spiritually incorporated into that one Body which had

40

already become a functioning reality. "For by one Spirit we were all baptized into one body."

I realize, of course, that many Christians hold to not one but *two* spiritual baptisms, the first administered by Jesus, and the second by the Spirit. According to this view, John the Baptist declared that Jesus Christ would be the baptizer; whereas the Corinthian passage indicates the Spirit as the baptizer. And because both persons cannot function in this role, there must be two spiritual baptisms: the first being an immersion by Jesus into the Spirit (the element), and the second an immersion into the Body of Christ (also the element) by the Spirit of God. Hence the claim that the former is an individual, post-conversion experience, while the latter is corporate and historical.

But I asked myself, "Is this necessarily conclusive?" I could not see it. I became convinced—and am still convinced—that there is one and only one baptism of the Holy Spirit. That great corporate and spiritual immersion occurred at the time of the Church's birth at Pentecost, and the subsequent outpourings at Samaria (Acts 8) and Caesarea (Acts 10) were extensions of this.

However, I had to face up to the honest objection raised by those who held the two-baptism position.

Are believers today baptized by Jesus into the Spirit as well as into the Body by the Spirit? Is the first an individual action to be desired and sought, and the second a fixed position into which all are introduced at salvation? And who does the baptizing—the Lord Jesus or the Holy Ghost? Or both? And what is the element—the Spirit of God or the mystical Body of Christ?

The more I thought and prayed and studied the question, the more it appeared to me that confusion could be resolved by viewing the Baptizer as the risen Christ *who acts through His divine Representative and Agent.* This Agent, in turn, immersed believing Jews and Gentiles into the one Body of Christ.

For instance, take the first two verses of John's Gospel, chapter four. In verse one Jesus is said to have made and baptized disciples. However, the next verse explains that the Lord did not baptize a single one of them. His close associates administered the rite. In other words, Jesus did it instrumentally.

In the same way He could have administered, from heaven, the great promised baptism at Pentecost, where the Spirit served as His Agent. Thus the Church, the Body of Christ, became a vital reality on earth. Not only is the Holy Spirit the great Uniter, but He is also the one who has animated, vitalized, and empowered this vast spiritual community through the centuries. He has made the Church the very dwelling place of the living God. "So then you are no longer strangers and aliens, but you are fellow-citizens with the saints, and are of God's household, having been built upon the foundation of the apostles and prophets, Christ Jesus Himself being the corner stone, in whom the whole building, being fitted together is growing into a holy temple in the Lord; in whom you also are being built together into a dwelling of God in the Spirit" (Ephesians 2:19-22).

In fact, I came to believe that the experience often described as "the baptism" is actually the filling of the Spirit. Clearly Pentecost fulfilled the prediction of the risen Lord Jesus when He said, "You shall be baptized with the Holy Spirit not many days from now" (Acts 1:5). Yet Luke's account of the phenomena that followed does not identify this as the baptism, but rather describes it as a filling. His words are, "They were all filled with the Holy Spirit" (Acts 2:4). And several years later, Peter referred to the same event as the baptism (Acts 11:15, 16).

This mighty visitation, therefore, combined both of these spiritual ministries—ministries which occurred simultaneously at Pentecost, as well as later at Caesarea (Acts 10:44-46; 11:15, 16). But because they both occurred at the same time, it does not follow that they are identical in their nature. *Baptism* and *filling* are not synonyms. The event was one; the resulting experience twofold. They were all collectively baptized, or immersed, into that new vital organism, the Body, but each was also filled individually.

For example, at my conversion I was born again, received eternal life, had my sins forgiven, and was saved by grace. This all happened at one time—when I received the Lord Jesus as personal Savior. Nevertheless, these four eternal benefits are not identical in their essence; each one has its own particular significance, though all occurred at the same time.

Now, some encounters with the Holy Spirit in apostolic times were dramatic, even spectacular. Luke's eyewitness reporting proves it. His use of the verb *fell* repeatedly underscores the point. The Spirit *fell* at Pentecost (Acts 11:15), *fell* again in Samaria (8:16, 17), and again in Caesarea, *fell* upon all those who were listening to the message (10:44). Other descriptive words are also employed, such as *poured out* (10:45), *came on* (19:6) and *shed abundantly on* (Titus 3:6, KJV). The New International Version renders the latter; *poured out on us generously.* Such vivid language conveys the dramatic suddenness of an almost overwhelming embrace, an accolade of power.

But the Spirit's reception and filling were not *always* dramatic and spectacular. Take the case of the Galatians. Paul asks them, "Received ye the Spirit by the works of the law, or by the hearing of faith?" (3:2). This is no dramatic, emotional description.

Furthermore, the text indicates that the reception of the Spirit followed immediately their exercise of faith in Christ. Nor can we forget the immediacy of Paul's words to the Ephesians, that upon believing the Gospel they were sealed (1:13).

5

All Believers Have These Benefits

After considering the Holy Spirit's relation to Christ, to the world, and to the Church, I now faced the challenge of considering the Holy Spirit's relationship to individual believers.

THE HOLY SPIRIT AND ME

I have already noted that before He returned to heaven, the Lord Jesus assured His nervous disciples that He would not leave them orphans. They would not be abandoned as helpless hitch-hikers on the highway to heaven. On the contrary, He Himself would come to them (John 14:18). This promise was fulfilled at Pentecost when He returned in the person of His Spirit to take up residence in the physical bodies of His own.

As I pursued this study, I felt a growing excitement.

As a Christian, I was certainly no orphan. My heavenly Father had poured upon me a veritable cloudburst of spiritual benefits. "Seeing that His divine power has granted to us everything pertaining to life and godliness, through the true knowledge of Him who called us by His own glory and excellence. For by these He has granted to us His precious and magnificent promises, in order that by them you might become partakers of the divine nature, having escaped the corruption that is in the world by lust" (2 Peter 1:3, 4).

"Everything pertaining to life" is apparently the provision found in the Comforter Himself.

Pondering further on this personal relationship, it became clear to me that some of the Spirit's operations were "invariables"—they apply equally to every child of God. Others are variables and do not apply to each. Some are fixed and permanent; others are fluid and changing.

Several ministries flow directly out of the experience of salvation, while others are dependent upon faith and obedience. All believers enjoy some, but only a few enjoy all.

Among these ministries are the indwelling, the sealing, the earnest, the anointing, and the Spirit's sanctification. Then there are others, such as the walk, the joy, the fruit, the filling, the power, and the guidance.

THE INDWELLING

The supernatural regeneration, described as the new birth, is accomplished by the Spirit of God as the agent and the Word of God as the instrument. Jesus declared, "Truly, truly, I say to you, unless one is born of water and the Spirit, he cannot enter into the kingdom of God. That which is born of the flesh is flesh; and that which is born of the Spirit is spirit" (John 3:5, 6). (Water is a well-known symbol of God's Word—I Peter 1:23 and Titus 3:5, 6.)

At this point, the divine Comforter moves both as the Quickener and as the Indweller. Faith in the Lord Jesus Christ is the sole condition. "If anyone does not have the Spirit of Christ, he does not belong to Him" (Romans 8:9). "Did you receive the Spirit by the works of the law, or by hearing with faith?" (Galatians 3:2). "Or do you not know that your body is a temple of the Holy Spirit who is in you, whom you have from God, and that you are not your own?" (I Corinthians 6:19).

THE ANOINTING, SEALING, AND EARNEST

"Now He who establishes us with you in Christ and anointed us is God, who also sealed us and gave us the Spirit in our hearts as a pledge" (2 Corinthians 1:22, 23). Here is a cluster of glorious legacies which are the common property of every believer. Even the carnal Corinthians possessed them.

The *anointing* of the Spirit heads the list, and is presented as accomplished fact. In the Old Testament, three classes received this "oil of gladness:" prophets, priests and kings. The ceremony of anointing with oil marked their inauguration to office.

In like manner each believer has received the divine anointing at the reception of his new life in Christ. Notice the words, "anointed us." This is confirmed by John's emphatic word directed to the newly born, whom he calls "children," or new converts. "But you have an anointing from the Holy One, and you all know. . . . And as for you, the anointing which you received from Him abides in you, and you have no need for anyone to teach you; but as His anointing teaches you about all things. . . . and just as it has taught you, you abide in Him" (I John 2:20, 27).

The anointing refers to the Holy Spirit's gift of discernment. The Holy Spirit within provides us with a discerning heart and mind, enabling us to distinguish the spurious from the genuine. Jesus said of His true sheep, "A stranger they simply will not follow, but will flee from him, because they do not know the voice of strangers" (John 10:5).

This calls for a dependent and teachable attitude on our part. It is possible to put away faith and a good conscience and thus to make shipwreck (I Timothy 1:19). Moreover, the young believer is said to "know all things." This refers to his capacity for all the truth of God. If I say, "I can see everything," I do not mean, of course, that every object on earth is now within the range of my vision, but rather that I have ability to see such if and when they do come into range. It is for this latter purpose that the same Spirit gives instruction through His own gifted teachers (I Corinthians 12:7, 9, 28; Ephesians 4:11, 12).

Although the initial anointing occurs at new birth, there are available to us countless after-anointings, or renewals, which we all need to appropriate (Psalm 92:10; 25:5). We are urged also to anoint our eyes that we may see (Revelation 3:18). It is the application of the oil that releases the benefits. So it is only as the Spirit is released and applied that His power and blessing are realized in our lives.

The *sealing* of the Spirit is another of the legacies that belongs to every believer. This is mentioned only three times in the New Testament. We are assured that we were sealed upon believing the Gospel and that this sealing extends unto the redemption of our bodies at the Lord's return. "In Him, you also, after listening to the message of truth, the gospel of your salvation—having also believed, you were sealed in Him with the Holy Spirit of promise. . . . And do not grieve the Holy Spirit of God, by whom you were sealed for the day of redemption" (Ephesians 1:13; 4:30).

When I arrived at this point three questions emerged: Who is it? Why is it? When is it?

The Sealer is God Himself, but He accomplishes this by His Spirit. The action is His—the Father's. The reason is found in the concepts of security and identity.

The sealing of Daniel in the lion's den (Daniel 6:17), or of our Savior's tomb (Matthew 26:66), as well as the letter of King Ahasuerus (Esther 8:8), all indicate the idea of the absolute security of that which is sealed. Furthermore, the seal declares ownership or title.

The story recorded in Jeremiah 32 is a delightful illustration. The imprisoned prophet was divinely instructed to purchase from his cousin a parcel of real estate. Shortly after this revelation, the cousin arrived and made the offer. Jeremiah paid the money and "signed and sealed the deed" in the presence of witnesses. Evidently the deed was furnished in duplicate: "the sealed copy," and "the open copy." Both of these documents were retained by Jeremiah's friend, Baruch. That deed was authority for legal ownership of that property. In the same manner our possession of the Holy Spirit is God's "deed" that every blood-purchased believer legally belongs to

49

Him. This is abundantly confirmed by I Corinthians 6:19, 20.

But there is one further question: *when* is the Christian sealed? Is it at or following salvation? Ephesians 1:13 states: "In Him, you also, after listening to the message of truth, the Gospel of your salvation, having also believed, you were sealed in Him with the Holy Spirit of Promise." This mighty transaction is consummated the moment one believes the Gospel of his salvation.

Finally, *"the earnest* of the Spirit," like the sealing, also is mentioned only three times in Scripture, in 2 Corinthians 1:22, 5:5, and Ephesians 1:14. According to W.E. Vine, the Greek word *arrabōn* (earnest) originally meant earnest-money deposited by the purchaser and forfeited if the purchase was not completed. In general usage it came to denote a pledge or earnest of any sort. In the New Testament it is used only of that which is assured by God to believers. In modern Greek *arrabōna* is an engagement ring.

Rebekah received jewels and garments from Abraham's servant in anticipation of her marriage to Isaac (Genesis 24:53). Jacob received wagonloads of goodies from Joseph in Egypt in anticipation of seeing him again (Genesis 45:21-28). So the earnest of the Spirit brings to the Christian a joyous foretaste of the glories that await his arrival in the Father's house.

THE SANCTIFICATION

Writing to his newly converted friends, Peter reminds them that they were "chosen according to the foreknowledge of God the Father, by the sanctifying work of the Spirit, that you may obey Jesus Christ and be sprinkled with His blood" (I Peter 1:2). Paul also rejoices over his converts when he writes, "But we should always give thanks to God for you, brethren beloved by the Lord, because God has chosen you from the beginning for salvation through sanctification by the Spirit and faith in the truth" (2 Thessalonians 2:13).

Remember the verb "to sanctify" simply means "to set apart for a special purpose." This too is a common possession of every believer in Christ. But how should we understand the appearance of the phrase "set apart" before the phrase "belief in the truth"? The answer lies in the convicting work of the Spirit which led the way to their repentance and regeneration. He had sanctified them in advance by initiating the entire work. Then, upon their conversion, He again had set them apart by giving them a righteous standing before God, based on the death and resurrection of Christ.

Writing to the Corinthians, Paul declares, "Do you not know that the unrighteous shall not inherit the kingdom of God? Do not be deceived; neither fornicators, nor idolaters, nor adulterers, nor effeminate, nor homosexuals, nor thieves, nor the covetous, nor drunkards, nor revilers, nor swindlers, shall inherit the kingdom of God. And such were some of you; but you were washed, but you were sanctified, but you were justified in the name of the Lord Jesus Christ, and in the Spirit of God" (I Corinthians 6:9-11).

Notice especially the order of the verbs in verse eleven—washed, sanctified, justified—three glorious absolutes, fixed and unchanging, which describe our position before God.

The other side of that coin concerns the believer's condition before men. We all need to be progressively sanctified by the Word and Spirit of God day by day. "But we all, with unveiled face beholding as in a mirror the glory of the Lord, are being transformed into the same image from glory to glory, just as from the Lord, the Spirit" (2 Corinthians 3:18).

Thus it appears that every true believer on Jesus Christ is indwelt, sealed, enjoys the earnest, is anointed, sanctified, and baptized by the Spirit into the Body on the sole ground of his saving relationship with God. These are invariables possessed by all Christians. They accompany our regeneration and assure us of our position as the children of God.

6

Only Some Enjoy the Added Benefits

My library is small—less than fifteen hundred books. But occasionally when friends step into my study they will turn to me with that embarrassing question, "How many of these have you read?"

Those books are available to me at all times. But to take advantage of their wisdom I must exert myself to open and read them. Likewise there are ministries of the Holy Spirit that become ours only as we lay hold on them. To these we now turn with the hope that we shall really possess our possessions.

In his letter to the Philippians Paul urges us to approve the things that are excellent (1:10). The marginal reading in the NASB provides an alternate rendering, "distinguish between the things which differ." The New

English Bible translates this as "the gift of true discrimination."

The more I study the Holy Scripture, the more conscious I am that we need this gift of discrimination in order to understand the delicate balance between truths which may appear contradictory and paradoxical, but when rightly viewed become complementary and explanatory. This certainly is true with the multiple ministries of the Holy Spirit.

For example, though each Christian is indwelt, he is commanded to be filled. Each is sealed, though he is warned not to grieve the Spirit. Each is anointed, yet he is urged to pray in the Holy Ghost. Each is regenerated and renewed, and yet he is commanded to walk in the Spirit. The joy, power, guidance, and the ninefold fruit are also glorious possibilities that beckon us onward to a Christ-filled maturity.

GUIDANCE OF THE SPIRIT

During the forty years of Israel's desert pilgrimage God led them by the pillar of cloud by day and fire by night. Their eyes were fixed upon a physical object as they trekked to their promised land.

Today, however, we are led by a spiritual Guide to a spiritual homeland. In fact, God has given us *two* guides: His Word and His Spirit. These are complementary; not the Spirit *or* the Word, but the Spirit *and* the Word. The Holy Spirit always leads us in the will of God as revealed in the principles of Scripture.

Does the Holy Spirit guide us today? Most certainly— providing we are guidable!

Hear our Lord's promise: "When He, the Spirit of truth, comes, He will guide you into all the truth: for He will not speak on His own initiative, but whatever He hears, He will speak; and He will disclose to you what is to come. He shall glorify Me; for He shall take of Mine, and shall disclose it to you" (John 16:13, 14). Note the phrases, "He will guide," "He will disclose," "He shall glorify." How the Spirit delights in revealing to our minds and hearts the supreme excellencies of our Lord Jesus Christ.

He also guides us in life's daily routines, so that our decisions, attitudes, and walk might be under His benign control, and subject to the good, acceptable and perfect will of God. "But if you are led by the Spirit, you are not under the Law" (Galatians 5:18). On the contrary, He will not lead us into lawlessness, but into the light and easy yoke of Christ. "For all who are being led by the Spirit of God, these are sons of God" (Romans 8:14).

The story in Genesis 24 is a beautiful illustration. Rebekah, the bride-to-be, mounts a camel and sets out to meet her bridegroom-lover, Isaac. She follows behind the servant of Abraham. Rebekah personally knows neither the length of the trip nor the route to travel. But she knows the guide, and that is enough.

We know our Guide, too. He will not mislead us! He knows the route to our heavenly Isaac. Hallelujah! "If we live by the Spirit, let us also walk by the Spirit." And if we "walk by the Spirit you will not carry out the desire of the flesh" (Galatians 5:25, 16). The walk refers to our daily deportment—the joys, sorrows, duties, and pressures. If we grapple with these in the energy of the flesh, by our own puny strength, we will surely collapse in defeat. But if we face them in the strength that flows from the abundant power of God's Spirit, we will be more than conquerors through Him who loved us. His resources are available to us by faith.

THE POWER OF THE SPIRIT

When the risen Jesus breathed on His followers on that first Easter Sunday, He later also charged them to "stay put" until Pentecost. "And behold," He said, "I am sending forth the promise of my Father upon you; but you are to stay in the city until you are clothed with power from on high." And then, some forty days later, just moments before His ascension, He gathered them together, commanded them to wait, and repeated the promise, adding instructions for world evangelization. "But you shall receive power when the Holy Spirit has come upon you; and you shall be my witnesses both in Jerusalem, and in all Judea and Samaria, and even to the remotest part of the earth" (Luke 24:49; Acts 1:4, 8).

The people who heard these words were a small, nervous crowd in an intensely religious city. Government authorities had executed their leader only days earlier, and they, figuring to be next on the list, had gone underground for a full month. Not one held the slightest promise of missionary potential. Any missionary recruiter would have awarded them all a cold zero! As representatives of their Master, they were pitiful failures.

As I reread and pondered those amazing early chapters of Acts, I was freshly seized by the conviction that some mighty power had descended upon these same men and women—a supernatural dynamic that transformed them from timid sheep into courageous lions. Instead of hiding, they are now boldly witnessing. No longer running away, they are now firmly standing. No longer timidly whispering, they are now shouting their message from the center of townsquare! Whatever has happened to them?

They have been clothed! The Lord's promise of Luke 24:49 has been fulfilled. The word *endued* means "to put on, to clothe," and is the same Greek verb to describe John's being clothed with camel's hair (Mark 1:6), and Herod's being *arrayed* in royal apparel (Acts 12:21). But notice that the verb is passive. They were not told to clothe themselves, but to wait until they *were* clothed with power from on high.

The opposite of being dressed is nakedness. This may explain the difference between their pre- and post-Pentecost spiritual condition. "May the God of hope fill you with all joy and peace in believing, that you may abound in hope by the *power* of the Holy Spirit.... in the power of signs and wonders, in the *power* of the Spirit" (Romans 15:13, 19). "And my message and my preaching were not in persuasive words of wisdom, but in demonstration of the Spirit and of *power*" (I Corinthians 2:4). "For our Gospel did not come to you in word only, but also in *power* and in the Holy Spirit" (I Thessalonians 1:5).

Even our Lord Jesus, who was conceived by the Holy Spirit, did not embark upon His public ministry until He was anointed and energized by that same Spirit thirty years later. Only then, when full of the Spirit, was He also led and empowered to launch His mighty service to God and man (See Luke 4:1, 14). The same sequence applied to His followers. Although their regeneration had occurred earlier (John 13:10,11), they were not ready to embark upon their missionary service until they had received the Spirit in fulness and power.

What about you and me today? Isn't much of our "church work" little more than huffing and puffing of religious flesh? Have we fallen into the deception of ignorantly identifying our feverish activity with genuine Christian service? Like the old maverick Jehu, do we call attention to ourselves by yelling, "Come with me and see my zeal for the Lord," and then invite friends to join us for a furious ride on our religious chariots (See II Kings 10)?

Perhaps God would have us soberly re-evaluate our motivation, dynamic, methods, and goals. Flesh is flesh, even when it is pious flesh; "it profiteth nothing." The true dynamic of all God-pleasing worship and service resides in the indwelling Holy Spirit; the true goal is the glory of God. In the Spirit we discover "the surpassing greatness of His power toward us who believe." Here only we face up "to Him who is able to do exceeding abundantly beyond all that we ask or think, according to the power that works within us" (Ephesians 1:19; 3:20).

It is shocking but true that multitudes of today's Christians, as far as *experience* is concerned, are living on this side of Calvary but on the other side of Pentecost!

THE FILLING OF THE SPIRIT

Since I first wrote the Emmaus correspondence course, *The Holy Spirit at Work,* I have regretted my inadequate treatment of the "filling of the Spirit." My understanding was unsure at that time. I did not make clear *how* to be filled, and thus to obey the command. I would like to think that the Lord has given me more light during the last thirty years.

Take the instruction to the believers in the church at Ephesus. "And do not get drunk with wine, for that is dissipation, but be filled with the Spirit, speaking to one another in psalms and hymns and spiritual songs, singing and making melody with your heart to the Lord; always giving thanks for all things in the name of our Lord Jesus Christ to God, even the Father; and be subject to one another in the fear of Christ" (Ephesians 5:18-21).

We have noticed already that every believer is indwelt, but not every believer is filled with the Comforter. Otherwise this command would be pointless. These very Ephesians who had received and been sealed by the Spirit are now urged to be filled (Acts 19: 1-7; Ephesians 1:13). They are prohibited from drunkenness and exhorted to be filled and to demonstrate the filling by speaking, giving thanks, and submitting.

Drunkenness of course is an effect, not a cause. The boozer thirsts, imbibes and becomes intoxicated; then the alcohol takes control. The parallel holds good in the process of spiritual fulness.

There must be thirst, for apart from *this* there will be no filling whatever. We must cry with David, "As the deer pants for the water brooks, so my soul pants for Thee, O God. My soul thirsts for God, for the living God; When shall I come and appear before God?" (Psalm 42:1, 2).

Centuries later our Lord Jesus answered this deep longing, and the echoes of His shout are still resounding. "Now on the last day, the great day of the feast, Jesus stood and cried out, saying, 'If any man is thirsty, let him come to Me and drink. He who believes in Me, as the Scripture said, "From his innermost being shall flow rivers of living water." ' But this He spoke of the Spirit, whom those who believed in him were to receive; for the Spirit was not yet given, because Jesus was not yet glorified" (John 7:37-39).

The recipe for the Spirit's fulness is beautifully simple; it is still available today. Christ in glory is the inexhaustible reservoir at which we drink; the indwelling Spirit is the river by which we flow. The drinking brings the fulness, and the fulness brings the flow.

THE FRUIT OF THE SPIRIT

Spiritual fruit is not so much "doing" as it is "being." The works of the flesh—immorality, idolatry, sorcery, murders—are abominable activities of depraved minds and bodies. But the fruit of God's Spirit is the godly attitude of a redeemed heart. Fruit, of course, is the visible evidence of invisible life. The nature of the fruit depends upon the character and power which produces it. In John 15:1-10 our Lord declares, "I am the true vine, and My Father is the vinedresser. Every branch in Me that does not bear fruit, He takes away; and every branch that bears fruit, He prunes it, that it may bear more fruit. You are already clean because of the word which I have spoken to you. Abide in Me, and I in you. As the branch cannot bear fruit of itself, unless it abides in the vine, so neither can you, unless you abide in Me. I am the vine, you are the branches; he who abideth in Me, and I in him, he bears much fruit; for apart from me you can do nothing. If anyone does not abide in Me, he is thrown away as a branch, and dries up; and they gather them, and cast them into the fire, and they are burned. If you abide in Me, and My words abide in you, ask whatever you wish, and it shall be done for you. By this is My Father glorified, that you bear much fruit, and so prove to be My disciples. Just as the Father has loved Me, I have also loved you; abide in my love. If you keep My commandments, you will abide in My love; just as I have kept My Father's commandments, and abide in His love." And Paul completes the picture in Galatians 5:22, 23. "But the fruit of the Spirit is love, joy, peace, patience, kindness, goodness, faithfulness, gentleness, self-control; against such things there is no law."

Roots are the source of fruit. In the spiritual life, the source is the indwelling Spirit of God. Fruit is not the result of the Christian's self-efforts. It derives from the divine Indweller. The secret flows out of our Lord's declaration that demands our cleansing (John 15:2), abiding (vs. 4-7) and obeying (v. 10). The substance, or production, is found in the ninefold fruit—fruit which transcends all natural morality. This fruit so abundantly marked our Lord Jesus during His entire ministry, but especially during those tense hours preceding His death. In that Jerusalem upper room, within hours of His cross, He referred to the first three of this rich cluster: "My love" (John 15:9), "My joy" (15:11) and "My peace" (14:27). Despite the impending agonies, there was no panic; everything was in the Father's hand and under His control. And the other six virtues were richly manifested throughout His entire life by the power of the Holy Spirit who filled Him. How exciting to realize that as we abide in fellowship with Christ, the Holy Spirit will form Christ's own character in us.

THE GIFTS OF THE SPIRIT

Just as there are nine fruits, so there are also nine spiritual gifts. These are mentioned in I Corinthians

12:4-11. "Now there are varieties of gifts, but the same Spirit. And there are varieties of ministries, and the same Lord. And there are varieties of effects, but the same God who works all things in all persons. But to each one is given the manifestations of the Spirit for the common good. For to one is given the word of wisdom through the Spirit, and to another the word of knowledge according to the same Spirit; to another faith by the same Spirit, and to another gifts of healing by the one Spirit, and to another the effecting of miracles, and to another prophecy, and to another the distinguishing of spirits, to another various kinds of tongues, and to another the interpretation of tongues. But one and the same Spirit works all these things, distributing to each one individually just as He wills."

All the fruits are available to all believers, but the gifts are distributed to particular individuals according to God's sovereign choice. And all of these divine enablements are still available today.

Moreover, this list in 1 Corinthians is not an exhaustive inventory, for other spiritual gifts surface in the twelfth chapter of Romans and in the fourth chapter of Ephesians. But it is of prime importance to note that these are all present in the Body of Christ—the whole catholic Christian community—though not necessarily in every local church. Doubtless, however, each local assembly has some of them; but not all. Thus the universal church is the depository of all the Spirit's gifts, true unity being expressed in diversity.

The most obscure Christian is not overlooked, as Peter insists when he writes, "As each one has received a special gift, employ it in serving one another, as good stewards of the manifold grace of God. Whoever speaks, let him speak, as it were, the utterances of God, whoever serves, let him do so as by the strength which God supplies: so that in all things God may be glorified through Jesus Christ, to whom belongs the glory and dominion for ever and ever" (I Peter 4:10, 11).

PRAYING AND WORSHIPING
IN THE HOLY SPIRIT

Every Christian is obliged to engage in the holy exercises of prayer and worship, but "he that is spiritual" will aim to live his entire life in such an atmosphere. Jude urges us to pray "in the Holy Spirit" (v. 20). Writing to the Romans, Paul declares an astonishing truth; "And in the same way the Spirit also helps our weakness; for we do not know how to pray as we should; but the Spirit Himself intercedes for us with groanings too deep for words; and He who searches the hearts knows what the mind of the Spirit is, because He intercedes for the saints according to the will of God" (Romans 8:26,27).

Later, he directs the Ephesians to "With all prayer and petition pray at all times in the Spirit, and with this in view, be on the alert with all perseverance and petition for all the saints" (Ephesians 6:18).

Both Jude and Paul are talking about a special form of prayer—"in the Spirit." As mere men, we are ignorant, knowing not what we ought to request, and weak as well. In both areas we desperately need the all-knowing and all-powerful Spirit to inspire, empower, and direct our prayers. He who indwells us knows our deepest needs, and makes His own intense intercession directly to the great Searcher of hearts on our behalf.

Moreover, in the believer's struggle with those behind-the-scenes powers of darkness—those sinister and malevolent fallen spirits who would plot his spiritual overthrow—his feeble prayers require the mighty adrenalin of God's Spirit. Only when these prayers intensify into supplications and become the very pleadings of the Spirit Himself do they cease to be infantile cryings and become the potent commands of Omnipotence. How assuring to know our two unfailing Intercessors: the Lord Jesus at the right hand of God the Father, and the Comforter who lives within our hearts!

Worship, too, must be "in spirit and in truth." Otherwise we play the role of modern Nadabs and Abihus by offering strange fire on Jehovah's altar. (Read afresh this solemn account in Leviticus 10:1-5.) The *New American Standard* rendering of Philippians 3:3 is an enlightening improvement over the King James translation, "For we are the true circumcision, who worship in the Spirit of God and glory in Christ Jesus and put no confidence in the flesh." True worship is not the product of mere religious stimulation. It flows upward spontaneously from the indwelling Spirit Himself.

In an allied passage, Paul indicates that such praises at times may even by-pass the intellect. "I shall pray with the spirit," he exults, "and I shall pray with the mind also; I shall sing with the spirit and I shall sing with the mind also. Otherwise if you bless in the spirit only, how will the one who fills the place of the ungifted say the 'Amen' at your giving of thanks, since he does not know what you are saying? For you are giving thanks well enough, but the other man is not edified" (I Corinthians 14:15-17).

Here are two wavelengths—one from the mind, the other from the depths of the human spirit. The latter was doubtless communicated in tongues. But if the vocalizing were in tongues only, with no interpretation, the hearer could not be edified. But the thanksgivings were acceptable to *God* for He understood perfectly. So this kind of worship should be limited to private exercise.

7

A Jolting Question

It was a beautiful Bahamian morning as an evangelist friend and I strolled along the road east of Nassau. Our spirits were in tune with the Lord of the universe. As we discussed the progress of evangelism and the church, Mr. Martin suddenly faced me with a startling question. "Brother," he said, "did the question ever occur to you that the Pentecostal folk might have something we have missed?"

What's this, I thought, *a word from the Lord or a trap of Satan?*

Then this man of God quietly vocalized his inward reactions to his own question. "But they do seem to be theologically shallow, don't they? There are so few real

teachers, so few expository books among them. But
even so . . . "

I have forgotten my reply. But I recall, this jolting
question did not arouse any latent hostility in me. In
fact, it drew my attention to several questions that had
periodically danced on the back burner of my
consciousness.

A PENTECOSTAL WATCHER

For years I had enviously watched these Pentecostals plant themselves in a town, send down roots, grow,
and usually multiply quickly. I persuaded myself that
their growth was a result of genuine evangelical fervor,
blatant advertising, religious ballyhoo, and sen-
sationalism. For me, this accounted for the middle to
lower sociological composition of their assemblies—a
cross-section of the more emotionally unstable of the
community.

Yet I recoiled at the fundamentalist zealots who identified these people and their denomination as heretics.
"By this you know the Spirit of God: every spirit that
confesses that Jesus Christ has come in the flesh is
from God" (1 John 4:2).

Yes, I had some doctrinal differences with the
Pentecostals, but our areas of agreement greatly
outweighed our disagreements. To associate these
believers with cults such as Christian Science and
Jehovah's Witnesses is uncharitable and a monstrous
injustice, like condemning a man to a leper colony
because he had a deformed ear!

ENTER THE CHARISMATIC MOVEMENT

Then came the 1960s. Early in that decade Christians everywhere became aware of a burgeoning

phenomenon known as the charismatic movement. The movement's momentum cascaded over almost all denominational walls, broke out as a fire at some seminaries and even on secular university campuses, touching Christian fellowships of all stripes. Even the secular press took notice. As at the first Pentecost, many people raised their eyebrows crying, "What meaneth this?"

Many regarded this newcomer as old Pentecostalism in fresh clothing—perhaps a twin sister. To others it was an attractive cousin—less emotional and more refined. To all it soon became clear that the charismatic movement was not just a visiting relative, but a new family member come to stay.

Renewal was the watchword. Many nominal Christians awoke to a new dimension of spiritual joy. They talked of receiving "the baptism of the Holy Spirit." Tongues-speaking and prophecies marked their devotions. Prayer, church attendance, and witnessing for Christ took on new significance. Home Bible study fellowships sprang up everywhere, spiritual excitement was in the air. Specifically, charismatics accepted as a present day reality *all* of the New Testament spiritual gifts.

One of the most surprising features of this new development appeared to lie in the absence of any single leader heading it up. Almost every great awakening has marched to the drumbeat of an eminent and gifted revivalist. But this movement—at least so far—has been conspicuous for the opposite. To date no Goliath has appeared.

I decided to take a ringside seat, where I could watch, and perhaps even learn!

Most of my viewing has been through books,

magazine articles, newsletters, and personal interviews, plus attendance at a sprinkling of group meetings. At these group meetings I felt a warm spiritual spontaneity on the one hand, but an absence of in-depth Bible study on the other. The hand-clapping praises were refreshing; the Biblical nourishment thinly seasoned gruel. The glow of God's love was always there. The atmosphere grabbed me as soon as I entered the meeting, and lasted to the final "Amen!" The Lord was there pouring it in, and the people were there pouring it out.

I must honestly confess, however, that I winced from time to time when theological bones stuck in my throat.

The over-visibility of female leadership was one of those bones. Another was the tendency to spotlight human experience at the expense of God's Word. And again, the sharing time tended, on occasion, toward discussion of mere trivia. But I quickly add that these things probably reflect spiritual immaturities and should not diminish my appreciation of the people's love and sincerity.

The honest researcher first gathers the facts. Then follows the more exacting task of collating and analyzing the evidence in the light of objective criteria. He must discriminate between facts and feelings, and avoid emotional prejudice.

I could have joined the bigot brigade easily. But I decided to prayerfully seek anew the mind of God on the matter. I knew I must reinvestigate the New Testament teaching on the nature, place, and purpose of gifts and manifestations of the Holy Spirit. Stubborn data and well-documented historical phenomena began to put some of my preconceived notions under an uncomfortable strain. My heart cried out for honest answers.

Certainly the risen Lord had promised that after His ascension, His own would be clothed with divine power and that mighty signs from God would verify their message. This promise was abundantly fulfilled during the apostolic period by the apostles, and by common Christians, both men and women (Acts 2:17, 18; 21:9). The book of Acts crackles with the supernatural power of the risen and ascended Christ, as His Spirit-filled representatives assault the kingdom of darkness and snatch the devil's prey, sweeping them into the kingdom of God.

All of this, however, stands in embarrassing contrast to the post-apostolic and present day church life. The cynical onlooker cries, "How come?" That early Church wrestled, fought, conquered, climbed, and raced. Today's Church is anemic and paralyzed, confined to a wheelchair. How come? What have we lost? It is obvious that we have lost something. Or is it *Someone*?

My theological dilemma lay in whether the gifts of the Holy Spirit catalogued in I Corinthians 12 were permanent.

For answers I turned to a fresh reading of Brethren leaders like Darby, Kelly, Grant, Ridout, Ironside, Barker, Wolston, and Goodman. I devoured these books. What a grip these men had on Scripture! My soul responded with a new delight in the glorious person, power, and presence of the divine Comforter.

But when they dealt with the question of the permanence of the sign gifts, they took either a negative or an evasive stance. I cried out for a clear statement from

71

Holy Scripture to settle the question once and for all. But no satisfying answer came. In fact, most of these authors merely assumed that which demanded solid and supportive proof. Empirical arguments, after all, are no substitute for a decisive word from inspired Scripture.

Yes, there was that nettlesome statement in I Corinthians 13:8: "Love never fails; but if there are gifts of prophecy, they will be done away; if there are tongues, they will cease; if there is knowledge, it will be done away." But as I pondered the verse in context (vs. 8-13), it was difficult to escape the conviction that Paul was contrasting the imperfect present with the perfect future, the childhood stage with the adult, the present obscurity with the future face-to-face consummation. Only then will these divine gifts cease. (See Critique at end of book for fuller treatment of this passage.)

THAT MARK SIXTEEN PASSAGE

In my search for Scriptural proof that any of these spiritual manifestations were off limits today, I became increasingly uneasy—even frustrated. I read Mark 16:14-20 a hundred times. "And afterward He appeared to the eleven themselves as they were reclining at table; and He reproached them for their unbelief and hardness of heart, because they had not believed those who had seen Him after He had risen. And He said to them, 'Go into all the world and preach the gospel to all creation. He who has believed and has been baptized shall be saved; but he who has disbelieved shall be condemned. And these signs will accompany those who have believed: in My name they will cast out demons; they will speak with new tongues; they will pick up serpents, and if they drink any deadly poison, it shall not hurt them; they will lay hands on the sick, and they will recover.' So then, when the Lord Jesus had spoken to them, He was received up into heaven, and sat down at the right hand of God. And they went out and preached everywhere, while the Lord worked with them, and confirmed the word by the signs that followed." Sure, many scholars do not accept the passage as valid, but it seems incredible that Mark would close his book with the abrupt trauma of verse nine.

Assuming the authenticity of this passage, I found myself figuratively joining that tense huddle in the upper room on that Sunday evening and hearing the Lord utter the Great Commission which all true believers accept as our marching orders for today.

Almost no one I knew brushed off the Great Commission as applying only to the apostles who actually heard it. But the five authenticating signs which were to follow believers—not just the apostles—are usually considered obsolete, having fulfilled their purpose in the initial experience of the Christian testimony. Any attempt to utilize them today, the critics claim, violates the principle of "rightly dividing the word of truth."

Here honest realism brings us to a skidding stop. Plainly, these five signs have not followed all of God's children. This fact has led many to the conviction that either our Lord never uttered this prediction, or else it was for the apostolic period only. I had to look further.

Nothing in the passage suggests that Jesus envisaged a brief initiatory period for the operation of these signs. Moreover, the whole context emphasizes faith. But the apostolic band was low on faith, for they "refused to believe" the report of Mary Magdalene (v.

73

11), and the report of the two Emmaus travelers (vs. 12, 13). Therefore Jesus "reproached them for their unbelief and hardness of heart, because they had not believed" (v. 14).

The message they were to preach called for belief on the part of the hearers (vs. 15, 16). Then came the forecast that "these signs will accompany those who have believed" (v. 17). And could we assume the corollary—that these signs would not follow those who believed not—even Christians?

Our Lord did not promise that every sign would accompany every believer. The statement is general.

Certainly these miracles did mark the apostles and their associates during the initial thrust of Christianity, as the book of Acts confirms. But where is evidence that the gifts were to be confined to that period?

Dare we limit the Holy One of Israel by dogmatically assuming that He pulled the "off" switch at the close of the first century? Even some of the most negative commentators grudgingly concede that God might so work today, but in heathen lands only, where the Gospel is making its initial penetration. My judgment was to keep an open mind, and to maintain a lively faith in the God of the impossible.

I have often been stirred and blessed by the judicious counsel and childlike faith of Anthony Norris Groves, the pioneer of Brethren foreign missions. His biographer, G. H. Lang, caught Grove's spirit when he wrote, "I have watched apostolic methods of evangelizing and church life succeed, as of old, in too many lands to be persuaded that they are unsuited to any one land. The Lord loves to do things differently from anyone

74

else, that the soul may say with comfort, 'This is the finger of God,' and may adore."

THE EBBTIDE OF MIRACLES
IN THE ACTS: WHY?

I now had to face another honest difficulty: what about the tapering off of miracles, especially in the latter half of the book of Acts? Does this indicate that miracles were on the way out, that God was preparing the stage for a new scenario? Were the miraculous signs reserved for Israel until the divine appeal to that nation had ended, and then the signs would not be necessary?

This popular notion strengthens the theory that all such manifestations terminated at the close of the first century. But a close-up examination reveals some serious flaws.

First, miraculous signs were certainly not confined to Israel. Look again at the story of Phillip's miracles in Samaria (Acts 8:6, 7). The Samaritans were not Jews. Or Paul's miracle at Lystra (14:8-18), and his healing ministry on the island of Melita (28:1-9). These people were not Jews. Moreover, someone was working miracles among the Galatian assemblies (Galatians 3:5). These people were not Jews. To top it off, we hear Paul declaring that the *Gentiles* were made obedient both by word and deed "in the power of signs and wonders, in the power of the Spirit," even as far as Illyricum (Romans 15:18, 19).

Supernatural signs were directed to *all* ethnic groups in order to demonstrate the mighty power of the living Lord.

Secondly, in the last nine chapters of Acts, seven "miraculous happenings" are recorded, three of them in the very last chapter (20:10; 21:4, 11; 23:11; 27:23; 28:5, 8, 9). True, they are less frequent than in the earlier chapters, but look, *not a single case of conversion is* mentioned in this same section. *Nor is a single baptism* recorded! This is startling, especially in view of the cloudburst of blessing that marks the earlier part of the history. Why this change? We dare not conclude that God withdrew his Gospel call to sinners at the end of the apostolic era.

How can we explain the reduction of miracles and the absence of recorded conversions and baptisms as Paul set off toward Jerusalem and Rome? The answer may lie in the question itself, namely that this beloved apostle *was* traveling to Jerusalem. From the data supplied by Luke, one might conclude that Paul's determined excursion was out of the "good, acceptable and perfect will of God" (See Acts 19:21; 20:22; 21:4, 11-14). Just count the warnings the Holy Spirit gave him, as well as the turbulent calamities that descended upon him. Did Paul deliberately "run" the red lights?

Perhaps here lies the reason that miracles decreased, that spiritual gifts seemed to ebb, and that conversions tapered off. How can a holy God bless and use to full capacity a servant who is walking in disobedience?

A similar choice by the Church may be responsible for its lack of spiritual power and effectiveness during those long centuries of the post-apostolic and medieval era. The Church was heading back to crippling legalism instead of bounding forward to the joyous liberties of Zion!

8

Imperfections of
Spiritual Recovery Movements

The other day I received a letter from a friend of many years. Tucked in the letter was this enquiry, "Could you give us your thoughts on the Charismatic Movement?"

In my reply I said that one can neither totally approve nor totally disapprove everything taught and practiced under this flag. The same remark applies to many, if not all, the renewal movements of history. Error has ever been prone to intertwine with truth, making it necessary for the godly to "have their senses exercised to discern both good and evil."

Who can deny that there were some elements of truth in the eccentric heresies that exacerbated the early Christian church? Sectarian protrusions often emerged in protest against what appeared to be a deviation from Scripture or current philosophies.

MONTANUS AND WALDO

Montanism and Waldensianism may serve to illustrate this. According to church historians such as Broadbent, Moncrief and others, the tendency to formalize everything in the area of collective worship developed early. Services were structured and brought under strict regulation. Thus enthusiasm was soon dampened and spontaneity smothered. These constrictions, however, brought about a rising tide of holy desire on the part of many for a fuller experience of the presence and power of the Holy Spirit, and a longing for a revival of apostolic preaching and practice.

About this time (A.D. 156), Montanus, a self-styled Phrygian "prophet," protested against the worldliness and stifling formalism invading the churches. At the same time he called for a return to primitive piety and the restoration of the Holy Spirit to His rightful place of leadership. He practiced a harsh asceticism.

The Catholic church viewed all of this as a threat to the authority of the bishops. Montanus and his eminent associate, Tertullian, certainly went to extremes, but they held to the essentials of faith in Christ. Their enemies, however, seized upon their views to vilify them and their cause. In spite of regrettable excesses, Montanism contained the seeds of a genuine movement toward the recognition of the Holy Spirit's presence.

Centuries later, about A.D. 1150, Peter Waldo led a vigorous reform movement within the Roman Catholic church which spread over a large part of Europe.

Finally excommunicated by the Pope, he and his followers resorted to a more serious return to the Scriptures, especially as these Scriptures related to personal self-abnegation and the preaching of the Gospel in the vernacular. Laymen and laywomen, whose hearts were hungering for spiritual reality, flocked to his cause, renouncing every other loyalty but to Christ and the needs of man. They launched a missionary movement that had at its very heartbeat a reverent obedience to the Bible, which had now been translated from the heavy Latin of the clergy into the language of the people.

All of this merits a place on the credit page of the Waldensian ledger. But wait a minute: What about these women preachers? And what about certain early compromises with the Papacy? Surely the debit column calls for some entries too. Though both Montanist and Waldensian reforms marked the resurgence of the Spirit of liberty and truth, they were not purist. Both of them sported blemishes.

A GLANCE AT MONASTICISM

The medieval church was also distinguished by the rise of the venerable monastic orders—Benedictine, Dominican, Franciscan, Augustinian, Trappist, and others. The founders of these orders were fanatically loyal to Rome, and relentless in their hatred toward those they considered heretics. Nevertheless, their disciples were often devoted monks, genuine in their faith, and obedient to the light as they understood it.

Yet who would attempt to defend from the New Testament the notion of the monastic system?

A GLANCE AT THE REFORMATION

And what about the Protestant Reformation of the sixteenth century? Is it lily white? If not, was God not at work in it?

Every historian sounds the high praises of Martin Luther, Melanchthon, and at a later date, Zinzendorf, Arminius, Zwingli, Calvin, Farrel, Knox, the Puritans, and the Huguenots.

What mighty reforms did God accomplish through these courageous and zealous men! Who will question the genuineness of the Spirit's mighty visitation as He breathed new life into those masses who for centuries had been smothered by the tyrannical papal system? As the fires of spiritual renewal were kindled throughout Britain and the Continent, God turned on the lights. As a result multitudes responded to the glow and warmth by bowing penitently before Him. It was kingsize spiritual renewal.

Yet as I reviewed the history of the Reformation, chills and shudders seized me. The pages are blotched and stained by episodes that flatter neither the Reformers nor their followers.

No one can read the accounts of the Zwickau "Prophets" and their religio-social excesses, of the Knights' War and their dirty politics, and of the Peasants' War and their revolting ambitions without concluding that plenty of embarrassing moments accompanied the reforms. The heavy backlash of Protestant hate toward their Roman adversaries provides plenty of demerits.

MORE REVIVAL VISITATIONS

Spiritual and social conditions in England were at a low ebb in the early eighteenth century when God raised up those fervent revivalists, John and Charles Wesley, along with the eloquent George Whitefield. The vigorous pietism coupled with the evangelical fire that distinguished these men issued first in the formation of the so-called "Holy Clubs," and later assumed a more permanent form known as Methodism. This spiritual awakening exerted a powerful influence throughout the British Empire and even in the United States. Masses were stirred to the urgency of removing social abuses, delivering the oppressed, introducing just legislation such as the abolition of slavery and prison reform, as well as evangelizing the unsaved peoples of the world.

But what of the theology of the leaders? Although the convictions of these pioneers were locked into the same evangelical framework, they differed sharply on some points. The Wesleys were convinced Arminians, while Whitefield held just as strongly to Calvinistic views. These differences, however, were not allowed to alienate or destroy their mutual love and confidence. Nor did the opposition and final rejection by the Church of England, wherein Wesleyism had been conceived, fail to extinguish its testimony. Methodism survived, despite its childhood illnesses, and became a sturdy church.

At a later date the Salvation Army took its rise, and gathering strength, reaped a mighty harvest for God, especially among the derelicts of the lower social levels. To this day the Army continues its great ministry of spiritual salvage. Uncountable thousands will rise up in the Kingdom and call it blessed.

But how many straight A's can we give to the theological tenets of either Methodists or Salvation Army? Many of us, I suggest, have serious doctrinal differences with both of them. But these differences do not prevent us from recognizing that "it is the same God which worketh all in all."

After all, God has had only one *perfect* Servant—His only Son, our Lord.

THE BRETHREN MOVEMENT

My background has been the Plymouth Brethren, and I owe them an inestimable debt. They taught me, nurtured me, endured and blessed me beyond measure, and I shall be forever grateful to God for the privilege of sharing their spiritual life and fellowship.

The Brethren are recognized for intense loyalty to the Bible as the infallible Word of God and to Jesus Christ as Savior, Lord, and Head. Their literature and missionary outreach have made global impact, far beyond what we might expect from such a small band. Their little assemblies are arsenals in which spiritual weapons have been fashioned, and from which good soldiers of Jesus Christ have gone forth to serve on spiritual battlefields everywhere.

The history of this movement, however, as chronicled by such authors as Neatby, Noel, Ironside, Veitch, Rawdon and Coad, makes for some lamentable reading. The story is punctuated by controversy, upheaval, and division. And these many splits have seldom concerned vital matters of doctrine, but rather have stemmed from ecclesiastical trivia.

As one of our Bible college professors facetiously said one day in class, "The Brethren are great folk, but they will divide over the difference between the northwest and the northeast side of a hair!"

God raised up the Brethren movement for the enrichment of the Body of Christ. But it, too, has proven to be an imperfect instrument.

The current charismatic movement falls into the same parade, sharing in the imperfections and immaturities, the blemishes and warts.

LOOK AT THE VERY BEGINNING

Throughout church history, every surge of the Holy Spirit has seen ugly manifestations of carnality, extremism, failure and evil. The perfect Worker has been working with imperfect tools. "Surely every man at his best," declared the Psalmist, "is a mere breath" (39:5). Or to change the figure, the Lord has piped but man has not danced. Or if he has danced, it has been a staggering performance at best.

Just because men and movements have staggered, swayed and fallen, we must not conclude that the Piper has not been present or that his music is off pitch. The failure rests totally with man.

Really, we do not need to examine the bleached bones scattered over the fields of history. We need only to return to our New Testaments and review the beginning of the story in Acts.

If anyone rejects a renewal surge simply because it is barnacled with doctrinal and behavioral errors, let him face these questions.

Was the Holy Spirit moving mightily during the period of the Acts? Yes!

Did any doctrinal perversions surface? Yes!

Any fleshly manifestations? Once again, Yes!

Do these conflicts cancel out the possibility that God was really active in such an incongruous situation?

83

The answer is a thundering, No! He was actively at work despite the circumstances.

Even my most casual reading of Acts shocked me with situations that bristled with problems. What about the city-wide police furor over the healing of the cripple at the Beautiful Gate (Acts 3, 4). This is followed by the deadly discipline that fell on the hypocritical Ananias and Sapphira (chapter 5). Next in line—the men who charged discrimination and cutbacks in their daily food allowance (chapter 6). These few cases focus on conduct. In later chapters we enter a more serious area of conflict: upheavals over doctrine, and serious upheavals at that. Check out chapter fifteen and the Epistle to the Galatians for details. The heat was on.

And then there is Paul's stubborn decision to go up to Jerusalem despite the tears of his brothers and sisters, and the siren soundings of his Lord (Acts 21:4; 10-14). Roaring through every red light, he landed in the clutches of a mob of infuriated Jews who nearly tore him limb from limb, and finally ended up serving a two-year prison stint in Caesarea (Acts 21:27-24:27).

Great men of God were Peter and Paul. How dearly loved and mightily used! What a whopping debt we owe them both. Who of us is worthy of wiping the dust from their sandals?

Yet at times they, too, were blundering flesh and blood. John Mark defected during his first missionary term (Acts 13:13). Peter took it on the chin when he was publicly rebuked at Antioch (Galatians 2:11). And even Paul missed the good and perfect will of God in his misadventure to Jerusalem. No wonder Paul reminds us that God has put "this treasure in earthen vessels, that the surpassing greatness of the power may be of God, and not from ourselves" (2 Corinthians 4:7). We are clay pots at best. The treasure He has put inside is what counts.

It became abundantly clear to me that fleshly extremes and sometimes lawless elements break loose in every corporate testimony, embarrassing and weakening its message. The lunatic fringe hangs on closely. Despite all this ugliness, however, God builds from His perfect blueprint. We should allow neither the glare nor the smog to so irritate our eyes that we fail to see the sun.

9

Is I Corinthians 14 a Museum Piece?

Old King Og of Bashan must have been a whopper. The Old Testament describes him as the last of the giants, though it does not mention his exact size and weight. But his iron bed was so large that, for years after Og's death, it was kept in a museum in the capital city of Rabbah. The fact that it was thirteen and a half feet long by six feet wide gives us a good idea of the King's massive frame. No wonder it became a curious antique. (Read about this in the *Living Bible* paraphrase of Deuteronomy 3:11.)

Chapters 12 and 14 of I Corinthians are not popular in certain circles today, especially the 14th. This latter chapter refuses to fit the twentieth century craze for programmed structures. It really is a large bed, for

it held up the whole Corinthian church, as well as all
of the other apostolic churches, back in Century One.
Not that they exactly *slept* in it. Rather, those believers
found support from it, and drew strength from its directions in their fellowship meetings. In so doing they
discovered that its governing principles were workable
and comfortable. Now read I Corinthians 14 for yourself.

NOW THAT WE HAVE READ
I CORINTHIANS 14

How was I to evaluate this chapter in the light of our
contemporary church situation? There are four possible viewpoints, as I see it.

First, I could regard the order indicated here as ob-
solescent, valid only during the primitive apostolic era,
when prophecy, tongues, and interpretations were
available. But this approach doesn't fit into today's
church scene.

A second view takes the principles of liberty and
spontaneity, as currently applicable, even though the
featured sign gifts appear to have long since
disappeared. It is argued that, because the Holy Spirit
is still here, the utterance gifts such as teaching,
singing, exhorting and praying may all be exercised
within the framework of this chapter. Hence in principle the order here is still valid, providing that
refinements and adjustments are carefully made.

A third position on I Corinthians 14 is what I call the
"beachcombers" approach. It walks through this chapter much as a beachcomber would stroll along the
seashore searching for shells. He picks up this one,
carefully examines it, shakes his head, and then tosses
the defective shell back into the sea. But the next one

brings a murmur of delight. He tucks it into the bag. Some are rejected and some are preserved. He who walks through this chapter, accepting one verse as having present day application, but rejecting another as a relic of the first century, will end up with a very small bag of salvage.

The fourth view is one of total acceptance. It regards all of these gifts, teachings, corrections, exhortations, and warnings as relevant to today's church.

Since I had promised myself an open-minded review of the subject I needed to exercise extreme care as I studied the Scriptures.

I realized, for instance, that few, if any, evangelicals would dare accept the first view, for it would make the inclusion of this chapter in Holy Scripture a mistake. These church directions would be superfluous; they would have no meaning for believers since that time.

The second view, however, was more moderating. It did not reject the guiding principles, even though it did refuse the specific sign gifts. But it left me with my own judgment to assess and apply these principles today. For example, right at the start we are urged to "pursue love, yet desire earnestly spiritual gifts, but especially that you may prophesy" (v. 1). Assuming prophecy and several other gifts listed in I Corinthians 12 are no longer available, what then should we "desire"?

In verses 24-25, Paul writes concerning a functioning church. "But if all prophesy, and an unbeliever or an ungifted man enters, he is convicted by all, he is called to account by all; the secrets of his heart are disclosed; and so he will fall on his face and worship God, declaring that God is certainly among you."

Could we expect these same results to follow the exercise of some lesser but surviving gift? Evangelism, for example? Not likely, in my opinion. Furthermore, in verse 26 Paul writes: "What is the outcome then, brethren? When you assemble, each one has a psalm, has a teaching, has a revelation, has a tongue, has an interpretation. Let all things be done for edification."

Now if revelation, tongues, and interpretations have disappeared by divine design, then the present day Church has only the two surviving gifts—singing and doctrine. Clearly the primitive Church enjoyed considerably more spiritual furniture than we enjoy today.

As to "revelation" (also v. 30), this may refer to fresh communication of truth directly from God. If so, then such revelations were definitely limited to the apostolic period and would not be valid today. However, the term might also apply to "a word in season" being divinely directed toward a particular circumstance. In this latter sense, God still makes His will known to His people. Maybe this was the better interpretation.

The more I read, prayed and meditated on these nagging Scriptures the more I sensed the inner voice of conscience speaking to me.

I remembered that when I taught pneumatology (the Holy Spirit) and ecclesiology (the Church) in our senior doctrine classes, I had to handle I Corinthians 14. To be honest, I was not comfortable with it. To be sure, I had some hard-nosed views about these statements. But some of these verses baffled me.

I just did not know what Paul was talking about. Nor was I anxious for students to detect my confusion—especially when some of them thought of me as an oracle. But more than once some sharp student would rise to the attack and overrun my shaky defenses. We had some real good-natured skirmishes which young people enjoy when they feel that they have stumped the professor.

As for the beachcomber view—the one who takes this approach becomes the self-appointed judge of which portions are acceptable for today and what are not. This is hazardous, for the fallible adjudicator may easily err in his choices.

For example, how inconsistent to insist that women be silent in the church (verses 34, 35), and at the same time dismiss the command to covet to prophesy and to not forbid speaking in tongues. Does not verse 37 prohibit all such attempts to evaluate these divine precepts? "If any one thinks he is a prophet or spiritual, let him recognize that the things which I write to you are the Lord's commandment."

In view of this authoritative statement, what other option is open? It appeared to me that we must accept the chapter in its totality, and yield to its principles. It is no museum piece. It is still God's perfect guide for the ordering of the central meeting of the local church today.

Taking this new view (to me) of the Scriptures I sensed fresh spiritual air, true body-life, and holy excitement. This was not the atmosphere of some deep and dank cellar, but a fresh sunny atmosphere where I could fill my lungs and laugh. Here I could sing, pray and listen to the voice of our living Lord as He speaks from His Word through the prophets, teachers, tongues-speakers, and exhorters. The unconverted are here arrested and brought low in repentance. The groanings of their convictions mingle with the praises of the saints as the divine maestro, the Holy Spirit of God, leads.

Abuses? Of course. Corinth had an overdose, to be

sure. But not once did Paul hint that the use of these gifts and spiritual ministries be abandoned because of occasional abuse.

Wherever there is liberty for the Spirit, there is also liberty for the flesh. And when the flesh, or even an alien spirit, invades such a meeting, the men in spiritual authority must intervene and rebuke in the name of the Lord. But to seek the remedy in resorting to a substitute ritual or "order of service" would reflect adversely on the Holy Spirit's wisdom and authority as spelled out in this neglected chapter.

Now it seems clear to me that First Corinthians provides us with the charter of the Church. It is as up to date as the day it was written.

BUT PROPHECY TODAY?

In this fourteenth chapter Paul gives prophecy the priority. Tongues are secondary. Only when tongues are interpreted do they rise to the prophetic level, for only then are the hearers built up (v. 5). Because so much ignorance and misunderstanding surround this ministry gift, let us take a close-up look.

First, what was a Biblical prophet? What was his role in the New Testament Church? Furthermore, inasmuch as he was frequently allied with the teacher, we should understand the difference between these two gifts. Again, was he always a foreteller? Or a forthteller only? Or both? Is this gift needed today? Dare we believe that God still provides it?

Let's begin with a definition.

The Hebrew word for "prophecy" signifies "what is lifted up, or a burden."[1] It also connotes "a flowing forth." Like an irrepressible inward spring, Jehovah's message overflowed from the preacher's heart and lips. The New Testament Greek word for "prophet" means "one who speaks forth, a proclaimer of a divine message," one who "speaks forth" for God. This minister is one who speaks on behalf of another at his behest.

HIS ROLE IN THE EARLY CHURCH

Two classes of prophets were active in apostolic times—those who were revelatory and temporary, and those whose ministry was more hortatory and permanent.

The first class often furnished fresh revelations of truth. "Surely the Lord God does nothing unless He *reveals* His secret counsel to His servants the prophets. A lion has roared! Who will not fear? The Lord God has spoken! Who can but prophesy?" (Amos 3:7-8). "And let two or three prophets speak, and let the others pass judgment. But if *a revelation*[2] is made to another who is seated, let the first keep silent" (I Corinthians 14:29-30). "Which in other generations was not made known to the sons of men, as it now has been *revealed* to His holy apostles and prophets in the Spirit" (Ephesians 3:5).

These inspired men received new truths from the Spirit of God, and communicated them to the saints. They enjoyed extraordinary insights into the divine mind. Their ministry was especially perceptive. The recurring phrase "apostles and prophets" underscores the temporary nature of their ministry.

Some prophets, however, were strictly predictive. Agabus for example. At Antioch and Caesarea he accurately forecast significant events. These projections identify him with this special class of foretellers.

93

Again, others were both perceptive and predictive. Certainly Paul, Peter and James were such men.

Neither of *these* prophetic categories is still operative. Raised up by God to furnish new revelations necessary to complete the full form of Christianity, (John 16:12-14), such ministry ceased when this was accomplished. Now the faith has been delivered once for all unto the saints (Jude 3), the canon of Scripture completed, and the job of those foundational prophets accomplished. "All Scripture is inspired by God . . . that the man of God may be adequate, equipped for every good work" (2 Timothy 3:16, 17).

Prophets appearing on today's religious stage and offering extra-biblical revelations are charlatans, and should be shunned as religious wolves. Paul warned that these would ravage the flock (Acts 20:29).

"PROPHETS AND TEACHERS": HOW DO THEY DIFFER?

In the New Testament prophets are not always packaged with apostles. Sometimes they are allied with teachers. "Now there were at Antioch in the church that was there prophets and teachers" (Acts 13:1). They ministered along with the teaching brethren in a harmony pleasing to the Holy Spirit and strengthening to the church.

Thus it appears to me that the gift of prophet and teacher are complementary. The one is necessary to the other for effective communication. The teacher speaks more to the intellect, the prophet addresses the heart and conscience. The teacher unfolds divine truth clearly and systematically. The mental processes are stimulated, the mind responds, and the fogs of confusion disappear as the light breaks through. "The precepts of the Lord are right, rejoicing the heart; the commandment of the Lord is pure, enlightening the eyes" (Psalm 19:8).

Then the prophet moves in. His penetrating look searches the depths of the soul. Probing the conscience, he asks, as it were, "You have grasped this doctrine? You now understand these truths? Very well; what are you doing with them? Are they making you more holy? More prayerful? More Christlike in the home, the office, the church? 'Unto whom much hath been committed, of him shall much be required.' "

The teacher *explains* truth to the mind; the prophet urges the hearer to *express* it in deeds.

Our Lord was both teacher and prophet. In the former role He explained everything privately to His own disciples (Mark 4:34). In the latter He probed a sinner's conscience and bared her past until she cried out, "Sir, I perceive that You are a prophet!" (John 4:19).

John the Baptist was a mighty prophet, too. But his powerful sermons really have little theological content. Perhaps there was little need of it, for he was speaking to people who were already custodians of all the riches of Old Testament revelation. But his Jewish contemporaries desperately needed the application of its ethic. Hence John's loud thunderings to the conscience.

"If all prophesy," writes Paul, "and an unbeliever or an ungifted man enters, he is convicted by all, he is called to account by all; the secrets of his heart are disclosed; and so he will fall on his face and worship God, declaring that God is certainly among you" (I Corinthians 14:24, 25). True prophesyings, therefore, when heeded, will yield edification, exhortation and consolation (I Corinthians 14:3).

ARE THEY NEEDED TODAY?

In this critical hour, dare anyone deny the need for such a ministry? The teacher's gift calls for the exhorter's gift, and closely allied with the exhorter is the prophet. These must all be exercised in a climate of genuine love and faithfulness, to the glory of God and the energizing of saints in the power of the Holy Spirit. Doctrine must never be divorced from practice; for *knowing* apart from *doing* may produce a first-class Pharisee. On the other hand, experience at the expense of theology may produce a first class fanatic! Maintaining the balance between teaching and experience guarantees spiritual health and maturity. We need the true prophet in this critical hour.

FOOTNOTES

1. W. E. Vine, (Revell) *Expository Dictionary of N.T. Words.*
2. As stated earlier, this may be a fresh revelation of truth binding on all saints for all time, or it could refer to a special word of comfort for a local need.

10

Prophecies and Tongues ... for Today?

Certainly prophets are not available in the primary
sense. The original prophets were employed with the
"foundation" and not with the roof of God's building
(Ephesians 2:20). However, there were both apostles
and prophets in a *secondary* sense even in New Testament times. Barnabas, though not one of the twelve,
is described as an "apostle" (Acts 14:14); so are Silas
and Timothy (I Thessalonians 1:1; 2:6). Likewise Judas
Barsabbas and Silas were "prophets" in the Antiochian
church whose ministries were encouragement and
strengthening of the brethren (Acts 15:32). These
prophets are examples of today's spiritual provision.

It appears significant that the gifts of apostles, prophets, evangelists, pastors, and teachers are bestowed

by the *ascended* Christ (Ephesians 4:8, 11). Now ascended and glorified, Christ continues to provide these love gifts for the perfecting of His own.

As we have seen, there are two types of prophets; those who were foundational and temporary and those who are non-foundational and permanent. There is every indication that the Head of the Church continues to provide permanent prophets today.

In light of the exciting possibility that Spirit-endowed prophets are still available to the Church, it is important to note two commands addressed to two local assemblies. "Pursue love, yet desire earnestly spiritual gifts, but especially that you may prophesy" (I Corinthians 14:1). "Do not quench the Spirit; do not despise prophetic utterances. But examine everything carefully; hold fast to that which is good; abstain from every form of evil" (I Thessalonians 5:19-22).

We must not toss off these words as being no longer applicable. If we assume that living in the twentieth century makes I Corinthians 14 obsolete, we must also be prepared to discard the whole package—verses 33, 34 and 35. But how can we possibly do this in view of verse 37?

I had to face the facts. We really cannot pick and choose. This chapter is not disposable simply because it contains some sticky verses.

The great emphasis in this passage, of course, is the edification of the assembly. And it is only by the communication of truth in the atmosphere of God's love that this can be achieved. Therefore, we are urged no fewer than three times to pursue love, and to earnestly desire the best gifts, especially to prophesy (I Corinthians 12:31; 14:1, 39). In so doing, we shall be desiring one of "the greater gifts."

The second passage indicates that prophets functioned in the Thessalonian church. Acknowledging the leadership of the Holy Spirit, these gifted men communicated divine truth through His power. It is possible that these utterances contained new revelations. But it seemed more probable to me that these Spirit-prompted prophecies did not involve fresh revelations, but rather fresh *applications* of truth already in their possession.

Thus this passage is particularly pertinent to today's situation. The Holy Spirit is the Spirit of judgment and of burning (Isaiah 4:4); hence we are warned not to "quench" His fire. Seeing the chaff in our midst, He would consume it, sometimes by bold and even devastating utterances from His prophets. And because it is the voice of the Spirit, and not merely a human opinion, the utterances are not to be despised.

It should be noted that the word is in the plural—*prophesyings*. Within the context of settled revelation, public utterances would emanate from several gifted men. Such a plurality would provide the check by which the hearers could test the validity of their messages, retain the good, and discard the spurious. "Every fact is to be confirmed by the testimony of two or three witnesses" (2 Corinthians 13:1).

Like many other Christians today, I am concerned at the ominous times in which we live. The tidal wave of religious liberalism, secularism, humanism, and demonic occultism is inundating Western civilization, threatening to undermine the foundations of church and state. Our churches and Christian homes are not insulated from the wreckage. We desperately need to hear what the Spirit is saying to the churches. And inasmuch as the Spirit uses sanctified men as His mouthpiece, we cannot dispense with the voice of to-day's prophet. We may not appreciate his sombre sackcloth or jolting messages as he shakes us out of our "ease in Zion" or topples us out of our "beds of ivory" (Amos 6:1-6), but we dare not turn a deaf ear, much less reach down for the stones!

Prophets today are calling us to rethink our attitude toward discipleship, the stewardship of money, time, our prayer life, morals, dress and self-discipline. Let us listen to the *source* of these voices, and realize that the living God is trying to get our ear. If from several directions searching messages are coming to us—messages that disturb, humble and plead—then let us not disregard these by assuming a head-in-sand posture, or, worse still, by attempting to behead the prophet himself!

God is still speaking through His messengers. Do not force Him to lament again, "I raised up some of your sons to be prophets and some of your young men to be Nazarites. . . . But you made the Nazarites drink wine; and you commanded the prophets saying, 'You shall not prophesy' " (Amos 2:11, 12).

TONGUES TODAY?

If prophecy is the major gift in I Corinthians 14, tongues is the minor. And because tongues carries with it the aura of the spectacular, it is more vulnerable to abuse. Hence the need for strict controls here. But let no one think that Paul is downgrading the gift. How could he? Its source was the Holy Spirit of God (I Corinthians 12:10).

The Gospels give the promise; Acts gives the practice,

and First Corinthians gives both the purpose and the perils.

"These signs will accompany those who have believed . . . they will speak with new tongues" (Mark 16:17). Here the Lord Jesus simply furnishes the promise with no accompanying explanation. The sign element is confirmed in I Corinthians 14:22, and is directed to non-Christians. The gift is available not only to apostles, but to believers in general.

The practice of tongues is recorded in three passages in the Acts (chapters 2, 10 and 19), and inferentially in one or two others (chapters 8 and 9).

It is significant that at Pentecost, the 120 were all vocalizing in tongues in the upper room before the crowds ever assembled. Gathered together, and in a sitting posture in a house in Jerusalem, the sudden descent and infilling of the Holy Spirit caused them to express their rapturous praises in other tongues. This sound, or the startling roar of the rushing wind, electrified the citizenry and attracted them to the epicenter of the Spirit's working (2:6).

The utterances were in a variety of languages, and this aroused the curiosity and amazement of the multitude. But these many languages were not evangelistic in their thrust. They were simply upsurgings of joyous praises, describing "the wonderful works of God" (v. 11). Compare Mary's Magnificat and Zacharias' Benedictus in Luke 1:46-55; 67-79.

In the Upper Room for the first time ever, the God of Israel was receiving praise in a proliferation of *Gentile* languages. This outburst was the divine sign that astonished the throngs in the street and prepared them for Peter's preaching, which brought three thousand souls into the reality of God's salvation.

On this occasion at least, the tongues were known languages. The listeners were residents of Jerusalem, not just visitors. The text clearly states, "Now there were Jews living in Jerusalem out of every nation under heaven" (v. 5). These people were part of the Diaspora. They had emigrated to the Jewish capital as adults. They were astonished to hear the local dialects of their early years coming from the lips of unschooled Galilean peasants. No wonder the crowd eagerly listened to Peter's explanation!

The second reference to tongues (Acts 10:44-48) concerns the second stage of the Spirit's great baptism when believing Gentiles were incorporated into the Body of Christ (ch. 11:15-18). Upon believing in the risen and glorified Jesus, Cornelius and all of his crowded houseful of friends (see 24, 27) were suddenly filled with the Holy Spirit. This filling was abundantly demonstrated when they all spoke out in tongues.

I couldn't help but realize that those who contend that glossolalia was simply a vehicle for evangelizing the lost are in a tight spot here. There is no evidence that there were any unconverted survivors to evangelize, and it is unthinkable that these new converts would preach to the seasoned Apostle Peter and his six Jewish associates! Yet they were all vocalizing, and without any interpretations. What is the explanation? They were simply directing their utterances to God and not to men. "The gift of the Holy Spirit had been poured out on the Gentiles also. For they were hearing them speaking with tongues and exalting God" (ch. 10:45, 46).

The same effect was demonstrated in the case of the

twelve Ephesian disciples. The story, recorded in Acts 19:1-7, is worth rereading. Only after these men had received the complete Christian message from Paul and been baptized and had received the laying on of his hands, did they speak with tongues and prophesy. The prophesying is a bit surprising, for prophecies are usually directed to people. But this raises the problem of the inappropriateness of new Christians addressing a veteran apostle. However, I remembered that prophesying was not always manward. In the Psalms of David prophecy is often addressed to God. The worshipful outburst of the aged priest, Zacharias, was also directed to God when, filled with the Spirit, he prophesied, saying, "Blessed be the Lord God of Israel" (Luke 1:67-75).

While these three passages provide concrete evidence of the practice of tongues, there are two other occasions when it also may have occurred. These involve the cases of the newly converted Samaritans and the newly converted Saul of Tarsus (Acts 8:17, 18; compare Acts 9:17 with I Corinthians 14:18). However, these are inferential only.

It is obvious from all this that tongues were not limited to Jewish converts or to the Jewish capital. This gift of the Holy Spirit was exercised in Jerusalem, probably in Samaria, in Caesarea and also in far off Ephesus.

What was the object of such a strange manifestation? As I explored the Scriptures, there appeared to be a threefold answer. As a gift of the Holy Spirit, tongues signify, glorify and edify.

First, they signify. They are intended as a sign. Our Lord had already predicted that "these signs will accompany those who have believed: in My name...they will speak with new tongues" (Mark 16:17). Later Paul declared, "So then tongues are for a sign . . . to unbelievers; but prophecy is for a sign . . . to those who believe (I Corinthians 14:22). This miraculous power of utterance makes non-Christians aware that *God* is present, just as it did at Pentecost. The crowd on that occasion was made acutely conscious that the God of Israel was in their midst as they listened to His glories being rehearsed in their own native dialects.

But no sign is an end in itself. It always points away from itself to something or to someone. For example, when the shepherds of Bethlehem were told by the angel that the holy babe would be found wrapped in swaddling clothes and lying in a manger, these unusual circumstances identified Jesus as the Savior announced. The clothes and manger were signs. The babe was the reality.

True tongues also magnify God, reach up and glorify Him. This happened in the upper room at Pentecost when the 120 vented their praises. It happened again later among the throngs on the streets. And it happened at Caesarea when Cornelius and his friends, in the flush of their new life in Christ and the infilling of His Spirit, magnified His name. Here we read that Peter and his friends "were hearing them speaking with tongues and *exalting* God" (Acts 10:46).

All this may be difficult to comprehend, and may even insult the intellect. But Spirit-produced tongues, never a status symbol for the exaltation of the flesh, appeared to bring worshipful release out of the depth of people's spirits. Even though the speaker's intelligence is not in gear, the upsurge of praise and petition reaches the ear of the great heart-knowing God because it is directed by His controlling Spirit.

I had to admit that this sounded far out at first. Questions at once arose as to how speech that is unintelligible to the speaker could possibly be glorifying to God. Then I realized that not all of our prayers in English always make perfect sense and glorify God. Moreover, I asked whether prayer-thoughts that successfully pass the checkpoint of our intelligence accurately express the real needs of our inmost beings. Do we really know the needs of our hearts? Can we fully express our real needs?

But praise God, there is One—and only One—who really knows our true needs. He is the God who "searcheth the hearts." Only One is competent to interpret and plead our concerns. He is the Spirit. Because both the Father and Spirit are divinely equal and divinely competent, they fully cooperate for our well being. The Spirit is not at all dependent upon our imperfect and bumbling communications system. He has His own, perfect in every detail. It never short circuits or suffers breakdown. His messages always flash through to Headquarters, and bring quick results. The communication media that He uses may be a tongue that He provides, or even a series of agonizing groans which cannot find expression in any words whatever. They simply "cannot be uttered." But because the pleading Spirit is their source and interpreter, they are effective and unfailing (Romans 8:26, 27).

The third purpose of Spirit-given tongues is that they edify. We may not fully understand it, but we must accept what Scripture declares.

"But you, beloved, building yourselves up on your most holy faith; praying in the Holy Spirit" (Jude 20).

"With all prayer and petition pray at all times in the Spirit, and with this in view, be on the alert with all perseverance and petition for all the saints" (Ephesians 6:18).

"If I pray in a tongue, my spirit prays, but my mind is unfruitful. What is the outcome then? I shall pray with the spirit and I shall pray with the mind also. Otherwise if you bless in (or with) the spirit only, how will the one who fills the place of the ungifted (or simple person) say the 'Amen' at your giving of thanks, since he does not know what you are saying? For you are giving thanks well enough, but the other man is not edified" (I Corinthians 14:14-17).

I came to believe that in each passage we are urged to pray in the Holy Spirit, but only in the last do we gain insight into what this exercise is. When Paul says he will pray and sing with both the spirit and the mind, he is not calling these one and the same utterance. On the contrary, these are two distinct spiritual wavelengths, at least in this context. He clearly indicates that blessing with only the spirit will not communicate anything to the one who does not understand (compare the NIV here), for the speaker is vocalizing in an uninterpreted tongue. How can the hearer sound his 'Amen' when he hasn't understood a syllable? Who is at fault? Clearly, the speaker. He has failed to interpret his own utterance (verse 13), and no one has come to his aid. God has understood and accepted his praise. But the other people have not been built up.

I noted in particular that there is no censure of this praying and blessing in itself. It is right and proper. But the place and timing have been wrong. Uninterpreted tongues apparently are not in order in the local church.

It seems clear that praying, singing, and blessing with the Spirit by means of tongues are on a different wavelength from utterances produced by the human intellect. Paul recommends both, provided that when voiced in the assembly, tongues be interpreted. "If there is no interpreter, let him keep silent in the church" (v. 28). And there are additional controls for public tongues when "the whole church should assemble together" (v. 23). The speakers are limited: "at the most three." These are to speak in turn, not in unison (v. 27). Order and self-control are necessary, with the spiritual upbuilding of the congregation as the goal (v. 32, 33). Furthermore, the Apostle Paul in verses 34 and 35 seems to prohibit women from participating audibly.

For private praying in the Spirit, regulations are less rigid. From examples in Acts, we have seen that this exercise was primarily Godward and inferior to prophesying. "For one who speaks in a tongue does not speak to men, but to God; for no one understands, but in his spirit he speaks mysteries. . . . One who speaks in a tongue edifies himself; but one who prophesies edifies the church" (I Corinthians 14:2, 4).

Self-edification is not as valuable as congregational edification. But it is not prohibited. When the speaker is denied the right to give a public utterance because of the lack of an interpreter, Paul suggests that he "speak to himself and to God" (v. 28). This indicates that the speaker is in control of his faculties, and also that he may exercise his communications in private. Paul doubtless refers to this kind of situation when he exults, "I thank God, I speak in tongues more than you all" (v. 18).

Those who practice private and devotional tongues, I discovered, often testify to the spiritual benefits— emotional release, lifting of burdens, and a renewed sense of the Lord's reality and nearness. Thus their faith is strengthened and their spiritual lives built up. No wonder this great chapter ends with the command: "do not forbid to speak in tongues" (v. 39).

But I also reminded myself that there is no spiritual gift that the devil cannot counterfeit. Our modern religious carnival abounds with false prophets. Demon-possessed witch doctors and the most obscure heretic may both speak in tongues. Just look at some of the anti-Christian cults.

Again, tongues may be psychologically induced by individual or group coaching. The Spirit of God has nothing whatever to do with this.

SUMMARY

Perhaps a capsule summary of my convictions may now be in order.

(1) All of the Spirit's gifts made available to the early Church are still available today in the Body of Christ.

(2) Part of the reason for their absence for centuries of Church history probably lies in the Church's failure to appropriate them. The long neglected truth of justification by faith was recovered by such an appropriation during the Reformation.

(3) While prophecy is a priority gift, tongues are among the minor gifts. The *gift* of tongues is given to only some and is for Church edification. But the *manifestation* of tongues is chiefly for private edification and is available to all.

(4) The indwelling of the Spirit applies to every true believer in Christ, but the filling of the Spirit is a

command, being frequently a post-conversion crisis that results in new worship Godward, and witness manward. Tongues may or may not accompany this infilling. The Lordship of Christ and the infilling of the Spirit are two sides of the same coin.

11

Must We Divide?

The answer to this question all depends upon the issues involved. If these issues concern vital truths, then the answer is a decisive yes. If nonvital, a definite no.

But what *are* vital truths? These are matters that affect the foundation of the faith. These cannot be altered, subverted, or abandoned.

THE WEIGHTIER MATTERS

Are certain Biblical truths weightier than others? Are not all truths equally important? No. In the human body various members and organs are vital and others are nonvital. Likewise in the Bible. Our Lord excoriated the Pharisees for majoring on minors in their application of the Mosaic law. "Woe to you, scribes and

Pharisees, hypocrites! For you tithe mint and dill and cummin, and have neglected the weightier provisions of the law: justice and mercy and faithfulness; but these are the things you should have done without neglecting the others. You blind guides, who strain out a gnat and swallow a camel" (Matthew 23:23, 24)!

In other words, their bigotry led them into the domain of the ridiculous. Their overemphasis on the ceremonial virtually closed their eyes to the moral. The inconsequential took precedence over the essential, the tiny gnat over the giant camel.

Foundational Christian tenets must include those truths that pertain to God, Christ, the Holy Spirit, the virgin birth, the full deity as well as the sinless humanity of Christ, the cross, resurrection, glorification and the second coming of our Lord. This foundation also embraces the divine inspiration of the Bible, salvation by grace through faith, and the reality of both hell and heaven. These truths are non-negotiable. Any who would deny them could scarcely be called a Christian.

When Paul warned the Christians at Rome to "keep your eye on those who cause dissensions and hindrances contrary to the teaching which you learned, and turn away from them," he was warning against antichristian teachers, as the following verses show (Romans 16:17, 18).

The same is true when he urged Timothy to "let every one who names the name of the Lord abstain from wickedness" (2 Timothy 2:19). Here Paul had in view men who taught that the resurrection had already taken place.

The most severe demand for spiritual quarantine came from the Apostle John who commanded that

"Anyone who . . . does not abide in the teaching of Christ, does not have God; the one who abides in the teaching, he has both the Father and the Son. If anyone comes to you and does not bring this teaching, do not receive him into your house, and do not give him a greeting; for the one who gives him a greeting participates in his evil deeds" (2 John 9-11). Clearly John considered "the doctrine of Christ" so vital that compromise was intolerable.

LET'S NOT STRAIN ON GNATS

On the other hand, some teachings in Scripture are negotiable. For example, we see differences on the divorce question, details of prophecy, baptism, church government, women's ministry, tithing, and others.

Despite the nasty carnalities, internal wranglings, and ugly excesses plaguing the Corinthian church, Paul never once recommended withdrawal. He censured and corrected. Over each abuse he cried, "I praise you not." But he did not, in spite of the conditions, call on the spiritual folk to pack their bags and get out. And even when the circumcision party had found a roosting place in the Galatian congregations, Paul refrained from recommending withdrawal. He expressed the wish that those in error would cut themselves off, rather than order the saints to do the cutting (Galatians 5:12).

In the Thessalonian church, some Christians were just bumming. A reproach to their Christian name and profession, these idlers were to be socially isolated as well as admonished. And all this with their recovery in view. Thus their sin was not overlooked but faithfully handled. But no division, please!

Paul urged Timothy to remain on in Ephesus to curb

certain teachings that had been creeping in (See I Timothy 1:3, 4). And among the assemblies on Crete, an assortment of rebellious men, empty talkers and deceivers, especially among the Jewish party, were upsetting whole families and had to be silenced by the elders (Titus 1:10-13). This was severe but necessary discipline. Still, there is no hint of excommunication. Genuine discipline calls for a balance between love for Christ and love for the brotherhood. Spiritual guardians certainly have their work cut out for them!

Even the doctrinal hassels over the law of Moses in the Jerusalem church failed to split that church. There must have been internal tensions aplenty, but no visible division surfaced. These acute differences actually gave them an opportunity to demonstrate brotherly love! This was not merely applying bandaids to festering sores, but rather displaying the love that covers a multitude of sins.

These early churches were far from perfect. Almost every one of them had problems of defective doctrine or defective practice, and these called loudly for correction. Separation, however, was reserved for thoroughgoing wickedness (I Corinthians 5:13). And this word *wicked*, by the way, is a strong one, often used to describe Satan himself (Matthew 13:38). When applied to man, it indicates that the human will is in rebellion against the known will of God. This disobedience is not a matter of mere ignorance, but of willful rebellion, which as the prophet of old warned, is like the sin of witchcraft itself (I Samuel 15:23).

Many true believers today are entangled in various doctrinal thickets, but must not be regarded as lepers to be sentenced to some ecclesiastical isolation colony.

Somewhere along the line they have been ill-taught—or just plain untaught—and like the godly Apollos, they need an Aquila and Priscilla to expound the way of God to them more perfectly (Acts 18:24-28).

Take the variety of convictions today concerning the ministries of the Spirit of God. Some godly teachers are convinced that the sign-gifts of the Spirit were retired at the close of the first century. Others, finding no New Testament support for this position, believe that they are still available.

Not only do leaders disagree, but also scores of laymen who form the mainstream of evangelicalism. The crucial question then is this: Are their differences so vital that there can be no "give"? Must our mutual intolerance result in polarization? Is it possible for lowliness, meekness, and loving toleration to so transcend these differences that the unity of the Spirit can be maintained in the bond of peace? (Ephesians 4:2, 3). Must godly Christians reject godly Christians because they cannot agree on this issue?

Surely the New Testament thunders, No! Should anyone challenge this, let him reconsider the gigantic threat to church unity that arose in apostolic times over the circumcision issue. Let him reread the divine solution in Acts 15 and in Galatians. Peter's climactic argument was an appeal to their common possession of the Holy Spirit, who had removed distinctions between believing Jews and Gentiles. "God, who knows the heart," cried Peter, "bore witness to them, giving them the Holy Spirit, just as He also did to us; and He made no distinction between us and them, cleansing their hearts by faith" (Acts 15:8, 9).

Christians on both sides agree that every true

believer possesses the indwelling Spirit of God at conversion. Otherwise he could not be God's (Romans 8:9). The basic difference is in the matter of a post-conversion experience, sometimes miscalled (I believe) "the baptism." A better term is "the filling" of the Spirit. But does this difference justify the civil war raging in churches around the country?

It is unfortunate that our verbal cannonading has exaggerated glossolalia out of all proportion. The gift has been given top billing! *Tongues* is such an explosive word that many Christians run for cover whenever it is mentioned. Others let loose a volley of condemnation. This latter reaction has sometimes caused me to facetiously remark that English tongues are far more dangerous than any unknown tongues!

"RECEIVE YE . . . FOR GOD HAS RECEIVED"

In Romans 14 Paul met head-on the differing convictions that prevailed among Christians then. Some of the Roman church folk had been committed Jews; others, profligate Gentiles. Matters of foods and special days were a powerful part of the Jewish life-styles. But the Gentiles couldn't care less. Both groups needed to exercise loving tolerance.

The vegetables-only man, for example, must no longer despise the vegetables-plus-meat man. God had received them both. The special-day man must not judge the no-special-day man. God had received them both. Foods and days had nothing whatever to do with the Lord's grace toward them. Because He had first received them, they must receive one another. Each had liberty to retain his personal convictions within the boundaries of brotherly love.

We must not forget that the matters discussed in Romans 14 concern things of moral indifference, not foundational matters of Biblical revelation. The distinction is important. Where foundational doctrine is the subject, we cannot take a *laissez faire* stance. For truth is not optional. Truth is to be obeyed. Not all Christians agree on secondary doctrinal matters. Take baptism, for example. Some believe in infant sprinkling, others in adult immersion. Major differences? Possibly. But one's salvation does not hang in the balance. Godly believers are on both sides of the question. Differences on baptism should not divide the Body of Christ. The same is true of other secondary doctrines.

DIFFERENCES, YET FORBEARANCE

Disagreement in conviction will lead, of course, to differences in practice, and this may create procedural problems. But should not the woman who covers her head when praying or prophesying be charitable toward the woman who feels such a covering is unnecessary? Should not the believer who takes communion every Sunday be tolerant toward the believer who feels that once a month is enough? Should not the brother convinced of the pretribulation rapture walk in love with the believer who is certain the church will be here on earth throughout the tribulation? Should not the tongues-speaking believer fellowship with those opposed to speaking in tongues? And vice versa?

If tongues are used by one believer in his private devotions only, surely there should be no problem. And if tongues are manifested in the public assembly of the saints, the church elders should be alert to the controls outlined in I Corinthians 14. No Christian who takes

117

this chapter seriously would have reason to complain if the stated regulations were firmly and fairly applied. Fear of abuse is no reason to abandon the clear-cut "commandments of the Lord" (v. 37) concerning prophesyings, tongues, and interpretation, any more than to abolish the communion because some of the Corinthians were getting drunk at the Lord's table.

FOUR ESSENTIAL ELEMENTS

The New Testament provides four indispensable principles for maintaining practical Christian fellowship. If these are adopted and applied, they will defuse any threatening situation.

1. "Let all things be done for edification" (I Corinthians 14:26).

2. "Let all things be done properly and in an orderly manner" (I Corinthians 14:40).

3. "Let all that you do be done in love" (I Corinthians 16:14).

4. "Do all to the glory of God" (I Corinthians 10:31).

The *first* of these principles concerns the function of utterance gifts in corporate church life. Contributions of psalms, teachings, tongues, revelations, and interpretations are allowable, as the Spirit leads the various believers.

However, abuse is a danger. For wherever the door is opened to liberty and spontaneity, Old Man Carnality may seize the opportunity for self-display. What if fleshly and ungifted persons cavort about and turn the meeting into a religious jamboree? Biblical brakes must be applied. Every utterance must issue in edification. This liberty of worship and teaching is to be exercised only if it brings spiritual upbuilding to the listeners. Where edification is lacking, local shepherds must apply the firm discipline of reproof and restraint.

The *second* principle reinforces this. Everything is to be conducted in a fitting and orderly manner. This does not mean a preprogrammed service, of course, for such would neutralize the whole spirit of this charter chapter (I Corinthians 14). But it does mean that propriety must be wedded to spontaneity, order to vitality. No room here for the religious stuntman!

The *third* principle reminds us that genuine love is essential. This is not a sickly, sentimental slush that masquerades as the genuine thing, tolerating error as truth, wrong as right. Rather, love is that holy and glowing affection that marks the true Christian as a child of the Father-God whose very nature is love. All spiritual gifts must be exercised only in the climate of a love that suffers long and is kind, that vaunts not itself, and seeks not its own.

Fourth, all participation must have God's glory for its goal. Glory is simply displayed excellence. Christians attending such a fellowship meeting sense anew this divine excellence. They will want to worship. Instead of returning to their homes empty, or muttering criticisms over the dull and lifeless service, they will be spiritually "walking, leaping and praising" the God who has shone into their hearts, to give the light of the knowledge of the glory of God in the face of Jesus Christ.

With these four basic guidelines firmly staked out—edification, order, love and godly motivation—our fellowship can be open and joyful. With the Holy Spirit as the divine Maestro, the entire orchestra of utterance gifts will respond with spiritual order and precision, producing harmonious worship Godward and suitable ministry manward.

Anachronistic? Idealistic? Impractical? No, indeed! An exciting spiritual dimension is within the reach of every Christian community that is ready to tune up all the instruments and seat all the musicians.

But we must trust the heavenly Conductor to lead according to His skill and wisdom. Let us play under His direction. Let Him wield His own baton.

We must not quarrel!

We shall not divide!

12

Don't Ignore the Amber Lights

All kinds of drivers crowd our highways. Most are responsible citizens. Despite the rules of the road, however, there are the speed demons, the snails, and the odd assortment of slaphappy hot rodders. Hence the ever present need for traffic cops, warning signs, plus green, amber and red lights.

The same is true in a religious sense. These are a few caution lights for both charismatic and non-charismatic believers.

CAUTIONS FOR THE CHARISMATICS

God speaks to men chiefly through His Word and His Spirit. The former is the external witness; the latter, the internal witness. The Word is objective; the Spirit, subjective.

The Word of God provides the tracks for the train; the Spirit puts steam into the cylinders.

Spiritual balance calls for both sound doctrine and vital experience. If experience is overemphasized, there is danger of blowing up; if doctrine is overemphasized, of drying up. The former can make a red-hot fanatic; the latter, an ice-cold Pharisee.

A large shiny locomotive sits on a special set of rails just outside one of the large stations in Winnipeg, Manitoba. It is a showpiece, recalling the days when railroads were at their peak.

Farther west, another locomotive lies overturned along an abandoned track somewhere in the Rockies of British Columbia. Now covered by vegetation, the wreck has been left as a warning of someone's carelessness.

The Winnipeg locomotive reminds me of the well-taught, tradition-loving Pharisee—on the tracks all right, but going nowhere. He has neither fire nor steam. But the wreck in the Rockies warns of letting too much spiritual steam dislodge one from the rails of sound doctrine. The end is disaster.

Charismatics, it seems to me, are long on experience and short on Scripture. Extra-Biblical "visions" and "leadings" have sometimes resulted in wreckage. The Spirit of God never leads contrary to the Word of God, nor does that same Spirit ever replace the written revelation. We do not choose between the Bible and the Holy Spirit, but we rely on both the Bible and the Holy Spirit. The two always go hand in hand. Doctrine is wedded to experience, and experience to doctrine. Just as words require breath, so truth, if it is to be effectual, requires the Spirit to vivify it.

A few examples underscore this important principle. Starting with the darkness and chaos of Genesis 1:1-3, we read, "... and the Spirit of God was moving over the surface of the waters. Then God said ... " Notice the mutual activity of God's Spirit and Word. The same order marks the prophetic unfolding recorded in Ezekiel 37 where the same two divine forces are at work (vs. 1-14). This partnership appears frequently in the New Testament (John 3:5; 6:63; Acts 4:31, I Thessalonians 5:19-21). Balance is essential. Never downgrade sound doctrine. It is the boney frame upon which the flesh of experience must be draped.

Another amber light—the over-visibility of female leadership in the current renewal movement. The Bible spells out limitations in the areas of both prophesying and teaching. The humble and spiritual woman will have no ambitions to contravene the commands of the Corinthian and Timothy prohibitions (I Corinthians 14:34, 35; I Timothy 2:11, 12). These limitations, of course, do not contradict the Scriptures which open to her a valid ministry.

Emotionalism is another danger. Emotion in itself is neither evil nor objectionable. Our Lord Jesus displayed healthy emotion when He "rejoiced greatly in the Holy Spirit, and said, 'I praise Thee, O Father, Lord of heaven and earth, that Thou didst hide these things from the wise and intelligent and didst reveal them to babes' " (Luke 10:21). In holy anger He denounced those scandalous merchants and drove them out of the Temple. His tears over Jerusalem afford a striking example of His perfectly human nature (Matthew 21:12,

13; Luke 19:41). Furthermore, the fruit of the Spirit—love, joy, peace—does not emerge so much from the intellectual and volitional areas of personality, but is basically emotional, expressing the very character of Christ Himself.

Emotionalism, however, is something else. This is the uncontrolled agitation of mind and heart which spills over into excessive physical reactions. Here earnest Pentecostal folk have sometimes failed. This excess has often aroused negative reactions from the nonemotional observer, leading him to discount any true spiritual values that may be present.

The final caution light to our charismatic brothers and sisters would be the danger that lurks in so-called *spiritual pride.* Sometimes those who have experienced the Spirit's fullness tend to regard themselves as the Lord's favorites, and at the same time flatter themselves into believing that somewhere along the line they have graduated with highest honors. Religious smugness is odious. God hates pride, especially if it bears a religious brand name!

There is no room whatever for Christian elitism. Any condescending attitude toward another brother is abominable to God. If I think that I have outgrown a brother, and therefore stand taller, just let me graciously bend down to where he is, put my arm around him, and give him a loving hug. We must not be pushy, or preen our spiritual feathers as though only we have "arrived." "And what do you have that you did not receive? But if you did receive it, why do you boast as if you had not received it" (I Corinthians 4:7)?

Those gift-happy Corinthian saints were far from spiritual. They were aircraft loaded with fuel, with no flight plan! The possession of spiritual gifts carries no built-in guarantees of maturity. Such maturity develops rather from the Spirit's fruit—love, joy, peace, longsuffering, gentleness, goodness, faith, meekness and self-control.

CAUTIONS FOR NONCHARISMATICS

Brethren assemblies, and many other evangelical churches, reject the current renewal movement. Their reasons are often rooted in the expository writings of early Brethren giants. This heritage, like all crystallized tradition, has been accepted with few questions by succeeding generations. Challenges to these settled matters are usually resented, for they pose a threat to the average Brethren believer. He usually prefers a ready-made theological package over the demands of a personal investigation.

However, it may startle some of my brothers in Brethren circles to read the writings of Darby, Kelly, Wolston, Stuart, and other pioneers. These gifted teachers were not at all in full agreement with modern teaching on the time-order of the believer's reception of the Holy Spirit.

True, they disallowed the sign-gifts in today's church, but they were emphatic that the possession and sealing of the Holy Spirit does not necessarily follow immediately after new birth. Consider this quote from William Kelly, "To be born of the Spirit is totally distinct from the gift of the Spirit. There is no connection whatever between the two thoughts. Who can doubt every child of God now, every one that is called by God's grace since the cross, is brought into the membership of the body? Not one Christian is left out. I do not say that all saints enter at once; but that there is not a single Christian who is not, sooner or later, baptized by the Holy Ghost."[1]

This jolted me when I read Kelly's lectures years ago. Later Brethren writers, such as Grant, Mawson, Ridout and others disagreed with these earlier teachers. Somebody was wrong. Perhaps these good men also missed their way in other areas of the Spirit's ministries, particularly in the matter of the survival or the renewal of sign gifts.

Noncharismatic evangelical believers share general agreement with their charismatic brothers on the personality and ministries of the Holy Spirit. Yet they permit Him only minimal liberty in public church services. This limitation doubtless arises from fear of fleshly excesses. Credit must be given to the Brethren for insisting that the weekly worship hour for the Lord's Supper be left entirely unprogrammed, open to the liberty of God's Spirit to use any brother in the exercise of praise, hymn selection, and public ministry. This weekly worship gathering around the Savior's cross has been a mighty spiritual preservative against liberal decay.

Furthermore, recognition and encouragement by the Brethren of lay participation has paid off generously in terms of a healthy development of ministerial gifts. Sure, abuses of this "open" meeting have occurred. Inappropriate remarks have sometimes been voiced, the unaccompanied singing has been poor at times, and the praise meager; but the spiritual pluses have overwhelmingly outweighed the minuses. In the normal assembly for the breaking of bread, participation is hearty, healthy, and above all, God-glorifying.

The Lord's Supper is usually the only service where a worshipper can be certain of spontaneity and openness to the free leading of God's Spirit. Here and there, one may find a mid-week free gathering for prayer, testimony, and Bible study, but these are not so common as in the earlier days of the movement.

From all this I do not insist that the New Testament positively limits us to this type of church service. There are examples in Acts of more or less arranged meetings in which teachers led disciples in an atmosphere of relaxed formality (Acts 11:26; 18:11, 28; 19:9, 10; 28:23). Both types of service are needed for the full nourishment and development of Christ's sheep. A fresh balance between the arranged instructional service and the unstructured "Koinonia" gathering is sorely needed today by every community, both charismatic and noncharismatic. Such a balance, I am persuaded, would bring a surge of spiritual rejuvenation and power. A few noncharismatics, in their penchant for sacred tradition, have developed a liturgy which makes Spirit-directed spontaneity quite difficult. The minister often performs on cue, while spectators in cushioned pews passively respond. I am convinced that if Paul were nearby he would come up shouting, "Yet show I unto you a more excellent way." Order is no substitute for ardor.

Another caution for noncharismatics is the need to avoid a phobia mentality toward emotion. Controlled enthusiasm has a place in Christian relationships. Timothy was urged to "stir into flame the gift of God" (2 Timothy 1:6 NEB). The Romans were to be "aglow with the Spirit" (Romans 12:11 RSV), and the Thessalonians were commanded to "not put out the Spirit's fire" (I Thessalonians 5:19 NIV). Apostolic church gatherings were punctuated by hearty "Amens," transparency, confessions, and the holy kiss. Member ministered to member in an atmosphere of fervent love. Religious masks, as in the case of Ananias and Sapphira, were quickly torn off.

All this suggests the legitimacy of true holy zeal. Flash the red stoplight whenever religious wildfire threatens. But hold the green for the flow of heavenly excitement in the Lord. Otherwise the very stones may cry out!

The word *excitement* may turn off believers with phlegmatic temperaments, who have been reared in a conservative atmosphere. But even these will shout at a football game!

Vital Christianity, let us remember, is victory, not defeat; a feast, not a funeral; a glow, not a gloom. Joyous excitement should mark Christians, individually and collectively. Heavenly joy comes from the Holy Spirit to those in whom He dwells in fulness (Acts 13:52). A joyless world waits to see it! Yes, and to experience it. How long must that world wait?

A final word of caution. Don't get hung up on tongues. Noncharismatic Christians can be touchy, and some panic at the very mention of the word. Their nervousness derives from a fear of the supernatural; some even regard tongues-speakers as demon-possessed. Relax, brother! When we ask our Father-God for fish, He does not pop a snake into our open mouths. We can fully trust His good gifts (Luke 11:11-13).

To be filled and controlled by the indwelling Holy Spirit is supremely important. Not only are we commanded to be so filled, but we are also told to covet earnestly the spiritual gifts that He bestows, especially prophecy. If the Lord grants tongues, praise Him for it. This is one of His love-gifts for self-edification. Be sure to "forbid not to speak with tongues" (I Corinthians 14:39). In view of Paul's enthusiastic "I would that ye all spake with tongues," plus his "I thank my God, I speak with tongues more than ye all," I have secretly mused that he would have an extremely difficult time getting beyond the threshold of many of today's evangelical churches!

Let us avoid all attempts to direct the mighty Spirit of God. He is sovereign, free, powerful and unpredictable. He brings liberty. We are living in the last desperate hour of world history. The powers of darkness are poised to unleash their last attack against the living Christ and His Church. As never before Christians need to shout the victory, with the prophet of yesteryear, "Truly I am full of power by the Spirit of the Lord" (Micah 3:8)!

FOOTNOTES

1. William Kelly, *Lectures on the Doctrine of the Holy Spirit* (London: Geo. Morrish, 1915 edition), pp 31, 247.

13

He Touched Me.

"When you reach Seattle," came the voice over the phone, "be sure to call our friends, the John Kruegers. They are radiant believers, and I know that you will be mutually blessed. Here is their address. Be sure to give them our love in the Lord."

I reached for my pen as I hung up the receiver in that Los Angeles hotel, resolving to follow through on the suggestion.

"It is always good to meet new Christian friends," I remarked to my wife. She nodded her agreement.

After settling in our Seattle motel a few hours later, I picked up the phone and called the Kruegers. They somehow recognized my name and promised to call back that same afternoon to set the time when we could get together.

Half an hour later the phone rang.

"You will probably not remember me, but I'm Rich Gill who was one of your students in Toronto over twenty-five years ago."

"Rich Gill," I exclaimed, "why *of course* I remember you, and your wife, Chloe. How did you discover that I was in town?"

He laughed, "Jeannie Krueger just phoned to say that you had called her. We've got a lot of things to share with you of what the Lord is doing in our lives. Could we pick you up and take you to dinner this evening? And would you be free to attend a Christian rally with us afterward?"

The next several days were full. The Kruegers and the Gills outdid themselves in a cloudburst of kindness. Sightseeing, dining, sharing with one another the glorious reality of Jesus' love, attending meetings that were aglow with the presence and power of God's Spirit.

In both the Gills and the Kruegers we observed a spiritual vitality that aroused our interest and curiosity. And as our interest grew, so did our hunger. Would they share with us just how the Lord had led them?

Quietly they told us. It was a simple story of commitment to Christ, then some years following their conversions, of meeting the Lord in a new way, by being "baptized in the Holy Spirit," as they termed it. Despite my reservations about the terminology, we listened closely as they recalled the spiritual encounter which had issued in a deeper walk with God, power for witness, new joyful praise, along with the bonus of a new prayer language. We had heard such testimonies before, but this time it was at close range.

One thing was certain: these people were not religious kooks. Far from it! They were college graduates, quiet, socially adjusted, and active in the world of education and business. Their homes were happy, their jobs secure, and their reputations untarnished. Their spiritual lives demonstrated joyous reality.

On the afternoon before we were to leave Seattle, we all knelt in the living room to pray. During those moments of spiritual outpourings, hands were laid on me as Rich and Chloe implored the Lord's fulness of blessing upon our lives and ministry. Sensing the presence of the Lord in that room, we arose, brushed away our tears, and embraced one another in farewell. We knew that the Divine Presence would go with us.

The next morning, crisp and bright, we packed for our noon departure. With an extra hour before check-out, my wife and I spent a little more time than usual in our devotions. Afterward she remained in the room with a new book, and I chose to go for a walk in a nearby park.

My soul was unusually filled with a renewed sense of the Lord's presence. I was newly aware of an upsurging of praise. I strolled along the paths, and the welling up of God's love vented itself in song. As I lifted my voice in praise, I used words that came to me, accompanied by a sort of chant, that seemed to release appropriately the upflow from my heart. I was supremely happy in the Lord. If I could not praise Him, I would burst!

After some time, I rested for awhile on a park bench, where with no observing eye but God's, I buried my head in my hands and poured out my heart to Him. Some of the words were not in English. They were syllables quite new to me, yet they flowed like a well of water springing up into eternal life. There was no overpowering seizure, no panic; rather a joyous outpouring, partly in English and partly in a new tongue. The indwelling Spirit of God, moving upon my own spirit, was the Source, but my will was in control throughout. It was quiet, but real. The Lord met me in a significant way during that morning stroll in a Seattle park.

I have enjoyed the Spirit's infilling many times down through the years in the service of Christ, but something was different this time.

For two weeks I told no one—not even my wife, Louise. Perhaps I wanted to test the reality of my new prayer and praise language.

More likely, I was apprehensive about the repercussions that might follow, once my friends learned of my experience. I had read Dave Hunt's *Confessions of a Heretic*, and had been stunned by the sentence of excommunication he had received from the southern California Brethren assemblies. I surely didn't relish this chilling discipline for myself. I did resolve, however, that I would share the experience with my fellow elders of our local church.

The elders received the news graciously, with no censure whatever. They volunteered to keep the matter in strict confidence. This was not the first time these elders had heard of such a phenomenon. Several other believers in our assembly had communed with God in tongues in their private devotions.

Sometime after my disclosure to the elders, a brother pointedly asked me if I had ever spoken in tongues.

So now the news was out! And really out! It spread like wildfire throughout the country. Then came the coast to coast calls, even from Canada, along with letters of enquiry from many sincere friends. All received honest replies.

The backlash has been severe. Some churches, where I have enjoyed full fellowship and have ministered with wide acceptance, have tightly closed their doors. Among them are assemblies that God used me to plant in the earlier days of my ministry. Some were elders whom I had personally led to Christ, and even discipled into the ministry. I confess that this has brought deep grief and considerable heartache to my soul.

Can it be that evangelical assemblies which profess strict obedience to the inspired Scriptures are prepared to reject Paul's fervent cry, "I wish that you all spoke in tongues" (I Corinthians 14:5)? In view of his two statements, "I thank God, I speak in tongues more than you all," and "do not forbid to speak in tongues" (I Corinthians 14:18, 39), Paul himself would be shunned in these fellowships.

To date only one or two dissenters have sat down with me in serious discussion over the Scriptures. A few have indulged in verbal bombthrowing; others have contented themselves with more subtle innuendoes.

But not all have been hostile. Some old friends have expressed their love and confidence. Especially am I grateful for the Palm Bible Chapel, North Palm Beach, Florida, where I have had a full and satisfying ministry ever since the founding of the work years ago. These saints of God have abundantly confirmed their love to my wife and me. They have been a source of tremendous encouragement during the most traumatic year out of a half century in Christian ministry.

Their warm support has helped heal bleeding wounds.

"Let the righteous smite me in kindness and reprove me; it is oil upon the head. Faithful are the wounds of a friend" (Psalm 141:5, Proverbs 27:6).

Since receiving this new fulness of the Spirit I can testify to a new surge of love, forgiveness, joy, and calm. There is also a new priority in praise. All during the years I had *taught* praise as part of my theology. But my teaching on the subject far outpaced my actual practice. Daily devotions had always been loaded with petition; praise was meager. When I turned afresh to the Psalms, I saw David's constant upflow of praise. He urged me to join him, and the Spirit of God responded within. I donned "the garment of praise for the spirit of heaviness."

In addition to these urgings from "the sweet singer of Israel," there has been encouragement from groups of happy believers meeting in homes around the country. Our initial hesitation at the free-flowing services, guitars, tambourines, upraised arms, hand-clapping and "Praise the Lords" gradually faded away as the spiritual reality came through.

Yes, many of these new Christians are reveling in their new joy, though they may for a time display traces of immaturity and zeal without knowledge.

But is there a nursery where everything is done decently and in order? Only cemeteries can claim total orderliness. And who of us prefers a cemetery to a nursery?

They will grow in time, and become an example to all

of us by their joyous and steadfast faith. As the Holy Spirit guides us, it will happen!

Does this sound like an instant, problem-free victory I have found? I hope not. For I have problems, testings, and periodic defeats. But our Lord has only begun. And He who has begun a good work in us will perform it until the day of Jesus Christ. In the meantime His Word is true; His victory is ours today; His Spirit empowers, and His grace is sufficient. Hallelujah! Lord, I believe!

Appendix

A Current Pamphlet,
Critique of "What the Bible Teaches about the Gift
of Tongues"
By: C. Ernest Tatham

Because of the current interest in the charismatic movement, thousands of God's children are hungrily seeking answers that both conform to Holy Scripture, and which could also issue in a deeper spiritual experience. Multitudes have already become experientially involved. These testify to the enjoyment of new spiritual dimensions—deeper joy, love, boldness and power for witness. Others not involved are cautiously puzzled. Still others are hostile.

It seems that almost everywhere I turn today I am asked about this phenomenon. Surely enquiring Christians deserve solid answers.

Now, in offering a critique of a current paper on tongues, I should first note areas of solid agreement.

The article rightly urges that Scripture, and not experience, be the criterion of truth, and that glossolalia can be practiced by non-Christian peoples who are empowered by demonic forces which simulate the Holy Spirit. Again, the explanation of the true baptism of the Spirit is clearly furnished. Furthermore, I am glad that the author does not recklessly identify all present-day glossolalia with satanic counterfeit.

However, when this booklet states that there is no mention of miraculous phenomena later than I Corinthians, and that this proves that such phenomena were not operative beyond that point, we feel his statement is untenable. The Lord's Supper is also not mentioned beyond I Corinthians. Does this prove that it was not observed among later assemblies?

We shall examine three pivotal questions:

(1) Were signs for Israel only?
(2) Were tongues given for the purpose of Gospel communication?
(3) Does I Corinthians 13:8 confine miraculous gifts to the apostolic period of the Church?

1. Were Signs for Israel Only?

The treatise under review states that "Signs and miracles were always connected with Israel," (p. 9). This is quite incorrect. While signs were primarily designed for Israel, they were by no means limited to that people. They were frequently performed in order to bring conviction to the Gentiles. The value of a sign is its function in pointing to something or someone apart from itself. For example, Judas's kiss identified the Lord as the Man wanted in the garden on the night of the betrayal; it was the sign to the mob (see Matthew

26:48). In like manner, miracles were signs to both Jews and Gentiles that the living God was on hand to verify the preached message. Spirit-produced tongues were just one of these signs to unbelievers of all ethnic backgrounds (I Corinthians 14:22).

Acts 8 contains the story of Phillip's miracles in Samaria (vs. 6, 7). The Samaritans were not Jews.

Acts 14 contains the story of Paul's miracle at Lystra. These citizens were not Jews (vs. 8-18).

Acts 28 contains the story of Paul's miraculous healing ministry on Melita. These people were not Jews (vs. 1-9).

Someone was working miracles among the Galatian believers. These people were not Jews (Galatians 3:5).

In writing to the Romans, Paul declares that the *Gentiles* were made obedient, both by word and deed, "in the power of signs and wonders, in the power of the Spirit" even as far as Illyricum (Romans 15:18, 19).

Any attempt to confine divine miracles to Israel is disallowed by Scripture. Miracles are directed to *all* cultures as God's corroboration of the message. Miracles and signs were not only beneficial to men, but also confirmatory of the Evangel. After the ascension the disciples preached everywhere, and among all nations, "the Lord worked with them, and confirmed the word by the signs that followed" (See Mark 16:20; Hebrews 2:4). In the light of this, how can we assume that there was need of such evidential confirmation only to Israel, and only during the first century or so?

2. *Were Tongues Given for the Purpose of Gospel Communication?*

The pamphlet under consideration cites a three-fold

purpose for tongues, viz: (1) a sign; (2) communication; (3) edification.

In connection with the second of these it emphasizes the notion that at Pentecost "a group of untrained Galileans stood up and preached the message of God" (p. 21), and that they did so in a variety of languages that were perfectly understood. That the languages were intelligible, no one who reads Acts 2 will deny. But to declare that these Galileans were thus preaching the Gospel to the people is to affirm what the Scripture does not say at all. On the contrary, it simply states that they were expressing "the great things of God" (v. 11, Darby). In the same way Luke describes the outburst of tongues at Caesarea later on. He says that they were magnifying God (Acts 10:46). In neither instance were these tongues-speakers *preaching*. Glossolalia was *never* used for the preaching of the Gospel. If anyone cares to challenge this statement, let him produce the text that substantiates such a view!

Let us ask a question concerning the value of the outbreak of tongues in the upper room at Pentecost. The fact that the 120 men and women were speaking in tongues in the Jerusalem upper room *before the crowd ever assembled* is frequently overlooked. But Acts 2:1-4 must be honestly faced. Many opponents of glossolalia are silent on this point. Why?

If the purpose of tongues was to communicate God's message on a person-to-person level, then we must conclude that this upper room group were all preaching to one another! Furthermore, the newly converted Cornelius and his many friends (Acts 10:24 & 44-46), upon receiving the Holy Spirit and tongues, must have immediately burst out in preaching to Peter and his six Jewish companions! Is it not a bit difficult to imagine new converts suddenly preaching to a seasoned apostle! Such a picture is ludicrous. I submit that this is an impossible conclusion.

If these two instances of tongues-speaking did not take the form of preaching and teaching, then just what did it involve?

It is my conviction that the tongues bestowal was a vehicle of communication that was *primarily Godward*. In the upper room, as well as later on, the recipients were extolling their Lord and their God in the form of rapturous praises, doxologies, and adorations that transcended the normal levels of thought and speech. Perhaps a sample of this might be found in the adoring rapture of Mary's Magnificat (See Luke 1: 46-55), although there is no suggestion, of course, that she expressed this in any other than her normal language. But the content was undoubtedly of the same quality.

Tongues in the New Testament were preeminently *praise*, providing a vehicle for the expression of feelings, rather than thoughts, that emanated from the depth of the human spirit. Glossolalia involved "praying," "singing," "blessing," and "giving thanks" to God in the human spirit, according to I Corinthians 14:15-17. Of course when such benedictions were given *in the assembly*, an interpreter was required in order that the congregation might add their intelligent "Amen" (I Corinthians 14:16).

If it be objected that the twelve men of Ephesus (Acts 19:1-7) spoke not only with tongues, but also prophesied, and that this prophesying would necessarily constitute preaching on the part of these spiritual babes, we would point out that such vocalizings were not *always* manward. A concrete example of this is found in the exultation of Zacharias, when he, being "filled with the Holy Spirit . . . prophesied, saying, 'Blessed be the Lord God of Israel' " (Luke 1:67, 68). This prophesying was actually praise, and therefore directed heavenward. We suggest that the same applies to those twelve Ephesians.

On the day of Pentecost the 120 sitting in the house (Acts 2:2) were all filled with the Holy Spirit and burst out in fervent praises to God, in languages miraculously given them. Shortly afterward, the multitude, attracted by this outburst, quickly gathered. It was then that each national heard "the wonderful works of God" expressed in his own dialect, and was filled with astonishment. Thus arrested, he was prepared for Peter's convincing message. Now notice. Not one soul was converted through the communication of the tongues. This phenomena was simply a miraculous sign that God Himself was in their midst. It was not the tongues, but rather Peter's powerful sermon, delivered in the common *lingua franca* that brought them to repentance and faith.

Tongues were primarily Godward; preaching was manward. And both were Spirit-given.

3. *Does I Corinthians 13:8 Confine Miraculous Gifts to the Apostolic Period of the Church?*

The frequent answer given to this question is a decided affirmative. Other Bible teachers are just as emphatically negative. The former teach that this passage completely settles the matter as to the tem-

144

porariness of tongues, prophesyings, and miraculously-given knowledge. Such phenomena, we are told, were all terminated at the time of the completion of the canon of Holy Scripture. It was at this completion that "that which is perfect" came, and it was this that brought the Church out from childhood into adult status. She put away such "childish things" as glossolalia, prophesyings, and certain forms of knowledge. These "in part" communications were done away, and exchanged for full knowledge, and a "face to face" understanding of God's truth. Hence the miracles ceased about the time of the death of the Apostle John, around the end of the first century.

On the surface this reasoning may appear to be conclusive. But I suggest that such a view is quite superficial, that it raises more questions than it settles. We must face at least four serious problems if we are to accept this hypothesis.

In the first place, how could Paul—rather, the Spirit speaking through Paul—describe prophesyings as "partial" and "childish" when these were His very own gifts? The proponents of the completed canon view, in their zeal to downgrade the supernatural manifestations, appear to ignore the fact that prophecy and tongues were some of the distinct gifts of the Holy Spirit. "To one is given . . . through the Spirit prophecy, to another various kinds of tongues, and to another the interpretation of tongues" (I Corinthians 12:8-10). True: the latter were at the bottom of the list, and the Corinthians were abusing them. But this does not weaken the fact that these were God's direct bestowments, and not mere childish toys. The author states that Paul's reference in I Corinthians 13:11 concerns

145

only the manner in which the child *communicates*, and clearly identifies "this infantile level of communication" (p. 30) with the Corinthian glossolalia. But Paul describes this genuine glossolalia as self-edifying (I Corinthians 14:4), a desirable medium of thanksgiving (v. 17), and an ability which he enthusiastically desired for every one of them (v. 5)! Furthermore, how could Paul possibly testify, "I thank God, I speak in tongues more than you all" (v. 18) if this was a mere "infantile level of communication"? If this were the case, we would expect him to say, and to say it *sotto voce*, at that, "I am embarrassed to admit that I speak in tongues more than ye all"!

Spirit-given glossolalia was a means of communion between the believer's own spirit and God. Nor is Paul descending to any "heavy irony" (p. 22) in what he states in I Corinthians 14:2. He is simply contrasting the value of the private use of tongues with the public use of prophecy. The former was self-edifying; the latter, church-edifying (v. 4).

In the second place, if these divinely given means of communication, and especially prophecy, were abolished when the Church emerged from its spiritual babyhood at the expiration of the apostolic period, how are we to evaluate those prophetic revelations given to it during that so-called infantile period? For let us not forget that inspired prophets brought to those early Christians divine and oracular communications with the compulsion to obedience as the very commands of God Himself. "Do not quench the Spirit!" charges Paul, "Do not despise prophetic utterances. But examine everything carefully; *hold fast* to that which is good" (I Thessalonians 5:19-21). *Did all these*

Spirit-given injunctions become void and inapplicable within a few years? In view of the fact that at least some of these utterances were incorporated into Holy Scripture, such a conclusion becomes intolerable.

Let no one conclude from this that, because I reject the canon hypothesis, I believe that we still have inspired prophets today who are capable of giving fresh revelations as authoritative as the written Scriptures. I do not believe this. I do believe, however, that God still gives prophets in a *secondary and subordinate sense*, men who *apply* the truth to the conscience.

Thirdly, let us examine this theory in the light of the approximate date of the alleged coming in of "that which is perfect," and the "face to face" condition of maturity. It is insisted that this arrived at the completion of the inspired canon, which would be about the time of the death of the Apostle John, A.D. 96 or so. However, Paul plainly states that it was *his* ministry that "fulfilled" or "completed" (J. N. Darby's *New Translation*) the Word of God. This filling up of the divine revelation lay in the unfolding of the truth of the Body of Christ, the Church (see Colossians 1:24-26). *This was the final and culminating truth, the capstone of the progressive unfolding of God's mind, the revelation of the "eternal purpose."*

We do well to look at the datings of some of the epistles. According to *The New Scofield Reference Bible*, the date for both Romans and I Corinthians is cir. A.D. 56. Ephesians, Philippians and Colossians were all written four years later, about A.D. 60. Now, in which of these epistles does Paul unfold the unique truth of the Church as the Body of Christ? The answer is startling. He explains it in Romans and in I Corin-

147

thians, as well as in Ephesians and Colossians. If anyone wants to check this out, let him simply refer to Romans 12:4, 5; I Corinthians 12:12-31; Ephesians 1:22, 23; and ch. 3:3-11; Colossians 1:24-27. The Apocalypse, while certainly part of the inspired canon, and of priceless value, does not present truths which supercede or transcend the revelation of God's hidden secret regarding the Church, as made known through Paul and his associates. Hence, "that which is perfect," if it does not lie in the ultimate future (as I believe it does), *must have come at the very time that Paul wrote I Corinthians; for the Body of Christ is fully explained in the twelfth chapter!* But it is in this *very* chapter, as well as those following, that he also gives instructions concerning miraculous manifestations!

In the light of this, does not the whole theory collapse right here?

However, if this is not sufficiently convincing, and one insists that perfection did not arrive until Ephesians was written, then let him consider the following. It is generally agreed that Ephesians (cir. A.D. 60) is the Mt. Pisgah of New Testament revelation. Written some four years after I Corinthians, this great document declares that the *ascended* Christ (not the Jesus on earth) was still giving prophets (among other gifts) for the upbuilding of His Church (ch. 4:11-13). This makes it clear, of course, that oracular prophets were still functioning despite the loftiness and finality of the truths revealed.

I submit that the canon theory places a most unnatural strain on I Corinthians 13:8-13. The plain and simple meaning of this passage concerns the vivid contrast between the present partial, imperfect, and childhood state of things, and the eternal complete, perfect and adult condition. It puts time over against eternity.

But there is a fourth factor that deserves attention. If the gift of tongues and its concomitant gift of interpretation were permanently withdrawn some few years after I Corinthians was penned, then so was the gift of prophecy. The latter was the superior, and therefore the more desirable gift. "Covet earnestly the best gifts," urged Paul. "Desire spiritual gifts, but rather that ye may prophesy." And again, "Covet to prophesy." (I Corinthians 12:31; 14:1, 39, KJV). Here are three vigorous exhortations. And the fourteenth chapter provides the detailed regulations for the exercise of this gift in the local assembly. Prevailing misuses and abuses are rebuked and corrected, as Paul lays it on the line and applies the divine controls. At the conclusion he buttons everything down with the words, "The things which I write to you are the Lord's commandment" (ch. 14:37).

Now if we are to believe that these various gifts were all voided a few years after this, then indeed this fourteenth chapter can hold very little value for us today. It becomes pretty much passé. How then can we insist that the regulation regarding women keeping silence in the church still strictly applies? In the interest of consistency, should we not simply point out that this prohibition (vs. 34-35) applied only in apostolic times, but has no current application whatever. Furthermore, what becomes of Paul's stern word that the things he was writing to them were "the Lord's commandment" (v. 37)?

It is my conviction that we cannot dismiss large portions of I Corinthians 12 and 14 just because those believers were abusing the gifts which the Spirit had bestowed. These same Christians were likewise desecrating the sanctity of the Lord's Supper (chapter 11). But this provides no valid reason for us to abandon that sacred Supper!

No, the Word applies just as forcibly today as when it was written. "Covet to prophesy, and forbid not to speak with tongues" (I Corinthians 14:39, KJV).

10 EXCITING PEOPLE SHARE THEIR FAITH

Colonel Harland Sanders, *Finger Lickin' Good.* The founder of Kentucky Fried Chicken recounts the homespun philosophy and life of a man converted at 79. Cloth $5.95.

Patricia Mochel, *Each Day a Miracle.* A remarkable story about a young woman, wife and mother of two, in coping with cancer through confidence in God. Paper $1.45.

Baroness Maria von Trapp, *Maria.* The colorful account of the conversion to Jesus Christ and discovery of the Holy Spirit by the original Maria of *The Sound of Music.* Cloth $5.95.

Janet Lynn, *Peace and Love.* The famous figure skater recounts her struggle as a teenager with the disciplines of sport and her faith in Christ. Cloth $4.95.

Shirley Boone, *One Woman's Liberation.* The wife of famous singer Pat Boone recounts her experiences behind-the-scenes with her family. Cloth $4.95; Paper $1.45.

Michael Gaydos, *Eyes To Behold Him.* A student for the priesthood discovers a new life in Christ, healing for his eyes and an astonishing new ministry. Cloth $4.95.

Bruce Olson, *For This Cross I'll Kill You.* An astonishing story of a young man's adventure into the jungles and the conversion of a whole tribe of Indians in Colombia. Cloth $4.95.

Pat Boone, *A New Song.* More than a million copies now sold of this astonishing account of a famous singer's discovery of life in the Spirit. Cloth $4.95; Paper $1.75.

Herbert Mjorud, *Your Authority To Believe.* A tough-minded-lawyer-become-Lutheran-pastor-and-evangelist recounts his discovery of the power of the Holy Spirit in our day. Paper $2.95.

Barbara Evans, *Joy.* The story of a Lesbian's search for real joy and her ultimate fulfillment in Jesus. Cloth $3.95.

The Wonderful Way of Living

One of the most talked about inspirational magazines today . . . Colorful personality profiles . . . skilled analyses of world trends in light of the Bible . . . Poignant narratives . . . wide ranging reports on the latest in helpful books and records.

Membership in Christian Life brings you this exciting monthly magazine plus Ten Additional Bonus Features including discounts on the best in books and records.

ORDER NOW AND SAVE

☐ Yes, please enter a membership in Christian Life for twelve months for $9 (for foreign subscriptions add $3 per year for postage).

Name_____

Address_____

City_____State_____Zip____

☐ Enter or extend a two year membership at $16 (you save $2).

☐ Enter or extend a membership for three years at $21 (you save $6).

T01

Become A Successful Christian Writer By Mail

"Writing is a skill that can be taught and learned by mail," says Janice Franzen, executive editor of *Christian Life* magazine.

She should know. Every issue of *Christian Life* magazine contains articles written by men and women who have discovered writing can become a rewarding and profitable ministry.

GRADUATES SUCCEED

Graduates of CWI achieve notable success. Many have authored books as well as magazine articles. Others hold prominent positions in publishing houses and on the staff of Christian periodicals.

Christian Writers Institute
Gundersen Drive & Schmale Road
Wheaton, Illinois 60187

Yes, please send me without obligation information on how to learn to write by mail.

Name_____

Address_____

City_____State_____Zip_____